WEDDING WHOOPS

by

Reward James Akpiri

New York, New York

WEDDING WHOOPS

This book is published by
Reward James Akpiri

Email Contact:
weddingwhoops@gmail.com

This is a work of fiction. All of the characters, events and dialogue portrayed in this book are either products of the author's imagination or are used fictitiously. Any references or similarities to actual events, entities, real people, living or dead, is intended to give the book a sense of reality.

WHEDDING WHOOPS Copyright © 2018 by Reward Akpiri. All Rights Reserved. Printed in the United States of America. No part of this book may be used or reproduced in any form or by any means, electronic or mechanical, including photocopying, recording or by any information storage and retrieval system, without written permission from the publisher – except in the case of brief quotations embodied in critical articles and reviews. For information address the publisher.

ISBN: 978-0-69296145-2

ACKNOWLEDGMENTS

This book wouldn't have been possible without the help of my friends, my entire team, and my partners. Special thanks go to my ex-wife; without her, this project would never have been born.

To my mentor and Manager Mrs. Leila Steinberg, Professor Awam Amkpa from NYU, Senator Ben Murray Bruce, Phillip Trimnel, Dr. Chika C. Onu, and especially thanks to the 2017 Nicholle Screen writing award winner Vigil Chime. She gave me the traction to begin this project almost 10 years ago, my go to ACE. Also to Diane Brooks, my book coach, my friend for sticking with me throughout this whole project. She stayed with me for the years it took to get the book finished. To my other partners Mr. Kayode Michael Arimoro whose belief in this project made it possible.

To all my friends and family all around the world, who stood by me and supported me, and to those of you who did interviews on the streets of New York to bring *Wedding Whoops* to life – thanks

TABLE OF CONTENTS

CHAPTER 1		Bachelor Party Rumor: He Said, He Said
CHAPTER 2		What the Groom Doesn't Know…
CHAPTER 3		Can't Get You Out of My Head (or Bed)
CHAPTER 4		Don't Worry, I'll Be Fine
CHAPTER 5		Hangover
CHAPTER 6		One More Post and I'll Unfriend You
CHAPTER 7		Mother Says, "Not Her!"
CHAPTER 8		The Baby's coming!
CHAPTER 9		White Dress, Green Card
CHAPTER 10		Marry Me, Too!
CHAPTER 11		My Wedding Day Was Canceled Twice
CHAPTER 12		I've had it, you're OUT!
CHAPTER 13		Who's going to Pay Me?
CHAPTER 14		Fighting All the Way to the Altar
CHAPTER 15		Left in the Lurch
CHAPTER 16		Last Minute
CHAPTER 17		Better Late Than Never
CHAPTER 18		Take Your Time
CHAPTER 19		I Have Nothing to Wear!
CHAPTER 20		Whatever the Weather
CHAPTER 21		Venue Disasters
CHAPTER 22		Best Man, Worst Case
CHAPTER 23		Lazy Katie
CHAPTER 24		Didn't You Get My Email?
CHAPTER 25		Money over Matter

TABLE OF CONTENTS (Continued)

CHAPTER 26	Cold Feet
CHAPTER 27	Let the Little Children Come to Me
CHAPTER 28	Adult Children, Big Babies
CHAPTER 29	My Vows
CHAPTER 30	Music and Dancing
CHAPTER 31	Roses are Red, Violets are Blue
CHAPTER 32	Ring Bearer, Ring Loser
CHAPTER 33	Photo Dilemma
CHAPTER 34	Customs, Rights and Wrongs
CHAPTER 35	Lights Out!
CHAPTER 36	Mocking Birds
CHAPTER 37	Enough Food (Poisoning) for All
CHAPTER 38	Stained and Strained
CHAPTER 39	Insecure Bride
CHAPTER 40	Mother Outlaws
CHAPTER 41	Put the Past behind You
CHAPTER 42	No Seat for the Weary
CHAPTER 43	You're Under Arrest!
CHAPTER 44	Saying Too Much
CHAPTER 45	Cry Baby
CHAPTER 46	Know When to Shut Up
CHAPTER 47	Last-Minute Blitz
CHAPTER 48	Hair and There
CHAPTER 49	Judy's Wedding Blues
CHAPTER 50	Wedding Nut

INTRODUCTION

Weddings are supposed to be magical – the most exciting and memorable day in a couple's life. From the well-planned proposal to finding the perfect dress, we don't want *unwelcome* surprises, hitches or glitches! Only beautiful experiences that bring us closer to the one we love. But, we all have those cringe-worthy moments we would much rather forget: the loud argument at the rehearsal dinner, and the florist we speak to *every day* who shows up with daffodils instead of roses. No one wants a $5,000 wedding dress that tears at the seams the morning of the wedding or a band that plays the wrong processional on our first step down the aisle!

There has never been a "perfect" wedding, no matter what the bridal blogs say. The good news is, the things that don't go according to plan are exactly what make the day memorable. The accidents and personalities, the unplanned and unwanted, they give us the "perfectly imperfect" wedding we never dreamed of.

This is a book about brides and grooms, their attendants and families, the wedding-day vendors, officiants, and venues. All the stories are based on real events, but I have taken some creative liberties with dialog or scenarios to keep things lively. I've also disguised the names and places to protect the innocent! These stories are true, and I know you'll love them!

Here's a little something about me: I was a TV director in Africa, and I moved to America and had to pay the bills. To pay those bills, I did video recordings of weddings, both freelance and for big wedding companies. I do more than just videotape a wedding. I creatively interpret a couple's journey, sometimes beginning with their childhood and going right through the time they met, all the way to the "big day." In the process of shooting a wedding, I become an intimate eyewitness to a couple's interactions with each other, their friends, and family. Everyone tends to forget I am there after a little while; I can be like a fly on the wall. I see it all: joy, doubt, disappointment, fear – you name it. I've seen how emotions can ripple out like shockwaves all the way from wedding planning to the altar or the reception – and beyond.

There have been times when I could have shut off the camera, but I didn't. I trust my instincts to know when something important is happening. Once I shot a wedding where the lights went out, throwing the church into pitch darkness just as the groom was about to say "I do." I turned my camera's spotlight on the bride in time to catch a look of doubt and worry on her face. I could almost hear her wondering whether this was a sign that he was not "The One," or this wedding was not meant to be. She looked scared, and she shivered in the two minutes of darkness at the altar. When the lights came back on, her face transformed, becoming as beautiful and confident as ever. But, what was that wave of doubt? Will it come back to haunt her later?

I'm a filmmaker now, but I did not want to make a movie about weddings – something to be forgotten after a year or so. I didn't want to create an ugly reality wedding show which makes it seem like bad behavior or glamour are the most important things about a wedding day.

I am writing this book because I want to help couples prepare, not just for their wedding day, but for their marriage. I hope that people will learn from the experiences of others and avoid making some of the same mistakes in this book.

I have a personal reason for writing this book; I had two very challenging wedding experiences of my own during the first year I lived in America. It was a time of uncertainty for me, whether I belonged here and if I would make it. The experience brought me a great deal of shame and disappointment. You can read about it in Chapter 11.

If you are planning your wedding, I hope you will embrace the crazy, the unexpected and the un-wished for stuff that inevitably happens. Your wedding isn't about the glitz and glamour or having the "perfect" day. It's about two people joining their lives in this old-fashioned, newfangled thing called marriage. I hope you will do what makes you happy on your wedding day, but spend wisely so you don't run into the burden of financial bondage. I hope you will avoid comparing your wedding to others and just focus on making your own history.

Most of the stories are scenes I shot, and the rest come from a wedding officiant, friends, and family members. The stories speak for themselves, but I've added some "morals" at the end. After working at hundreds of weddings, I have seen how attitude – a laugh or a shrug for instance - can turn the cringe-worthy moment into something wonderful. I hope I can inspire you to let go of some of the pre-wedding pressure and lighten up! I hope you'll write your very own wedding story – perfect just for you!

CHAPTER ONE
BACHELOR PARTY RUMOR LEAKS OUT

This first story is a cautionary tale and comes from my personal and not professional experience. Most cultures observe the tradition of a bachelor party where men get together on or close to the eve of their wedding day. It is a celebration to mark the passage from single to married life; bachelor to husband. The groom's friends give him a send-off into the estate of marriage – a wild party that might include strippers, bars, secret locations, and activities that no one is ever supposed to know about. On this night, a single man is presented all of his possible indulgences on a silver platter. After this night, a man is supposed to say goodbye to temptations forever.

This rite of passage varies from culture to culture. Not all send-offs are wild and distasteful. Some traditions are decent and even solemn. A Hindu bachelor party is different from a Chinese or African or African-American one. In the United States today, the parties range from weekend-long blowouts in Vegas to an afternoon round of golf or even a camping trip in the mountains where the only wildness is the wildlife.

For the crazier parties, there is a "sacred" commitment that the partygoers will never tell anyone about what happened on the night of the bachelor party. Some of the details could ruin a relationship, break trust between couples, and even cause the bride to call off the wedding. So, here is Shaun, who finally made up his mind to put a ring on it.

Shaun proposed to Donna, his girlfriend of ten years. I was one of Shaun's boys -- a bunch of us who had all grown up together -- and we decided his wedding was not going down without a major bachelor bash for our boy. We were going to pull out all the stops: there would be ten strippers, for sure! There'd be enough liquor to turn any New York street into a flood, and a spray of dollar bills to give the impression that we were mini-moguls. Shaun had no idea about the strippers. He had given us strict instructions (from Donna) that there should be no strippers, but we ignored him and went full-speed ahead. We were going to send our boy into marital bliss on the bosoms of the hottest girls money could buy.

The night began with advice from us "marriage veterans." We all know how selfish Shaun is, so we tried to give him some insight into how to make this thing work out. First, we told him he had to listen to his wife and let her win the arguments. We told him to hand over at least 65% of the money he made to her. Shaun was good and listened to his "elders." The party was going great.

Some men had early curfews imposed by their significant others who were suspicious of bachelor parties. They followed the strict orders given to them, and the party broke up. We thought that Shaun had gotten through the night without getting into trouble. It wasn't until the next day that we heard how wrong we were!

After we left, the rest of the guys ushered Shaun to the second location of the night for the mother of all parties. Shaun thought he was going to see a friend who could not make it, but when Shaun got to the party, he couldn't believe the number of girls in the room.

The place looked like a strip club. Two girls were assigned to Shaun, and they immediately rushed over and started to take off his clothes. He sat on a chair, and the girls took turns giving him lap dances. Donna's warnings to go easy were definitely fading from Shaun's mind. Everybody shouted encouragement:

"Do it, Shaun!"

"Don't disappoint us! You're the man, Shaun!"

"Go, daddy! Go, daddy!"

What's a guy to do? He had liquor shoved into his hand constantly, and he was drinking heavily. The girls chased him behind the couch, where he let himself be overpowered. Laughing, the men threw condoms at him, and he had sex with both women. Afterwards, the women left, and Shaun was depressed. Everyone swore they would not let it get out.

In every gathering, there is a Judas, a snitch, a hater. The wedding was the next day, and sure enough, Donna found out about Shaun's indiscretion in the wee hours of the morning. She was awake, unable to sleep because she was so excited about her wedding. We never found out who called and told her.

The next day, first thing, a bridesmaid confronted Shaun. Next, Donna's two sisters charged at Shaun with tears in their eyes asking, "How could you?"

Then Donna's parents came, asking the same thing. When a video of the event surfaced on a phone that was circulated to Donna's camp, there was nothing left to deny. All Shaun could do was to admit it. In his drunken haze, Shaun wasn't exactly sure what he had done that night. Seeing the video proved he had stepped way over the line.

"I was drunk!" he said." I didn't know what I was doing!"

"It's over!" Donna cried.

Donna had waited for over ten years for Shaun, but this agony was no way to begin a marriage. Donna said she couldn't go through with the wedding, even if it meant she'd be starting over; even if they would lose the $25,000 they had invested. She couldn't trust Shaun again, and his pleading couldn't change her mind.

If this story doesn't send cold shivers down your back, I don't know what else will. If you're not worried something like this could happen to you – congratulations on your self-confidence! If you aren't shivering or if the story sounds like a good time, ask yourself if you really want to get married! You might want to keep with the tradition of a bachelor party, but if you know you are weak around strippers, find other ways to enjoy it!

    Stay in control of the situation at all times. Don't drink too much, and keep your wits about you! Alcohol is used as an excuse for infidelity all the time. Surround yourself with friends who share your values and who would not lead you into trouble. What kind of friends hire strippers you said you didn't want? Do these men have your best interest at heart? They may say that they only want you to have fun, or they may want to have fun *at your expense.* Your sad story will be their entertainment for years to come. Shaun regretted his bachelor party. It cost him the woman he loved.

CHAPTER TWO
WHAT THE GROOM DOESN'T KNOW

When two-love birds hold hands in the park or stand on the sidewalk kissing; when they gaze into each other's eyes in a restaurant, or he opens the doors for her, his protective hand on her back, you see the beautiful thing; that is a relationship in bloom. As time goes on, she begins to see how this man is a reflection of herself. He realizes that this woman can make or break him.

However long this lovely courtship lasts, the day the two say "I do" is meant to be a beginning, the start of life's journey. It is a turning away from the past and a bold step into the future. However, for this adventure to work, the couple has to be ready and willing to let go of the past.

I've heard dozens of stories about how brides and grooms "meet cute" and fall in love. On a wedding day, I spend hours with the couple and all their friends and family. I hear it all! Plus, I watch how people get along while they are posing for the camera, and there's a lot to notice in the candid filming. I get an insight into the couple's lives, and I get told lots of stories, which is how I heard the next story.

James and Antonia met in a bar on a blind date arranged by close friends, Prince and Mattie. Antonia was curious and optimistic about their date. When she walked in, James was dazzled.

"She is really outstanding," he said to Prince." I hope she likes me."

"She liked your picture. I sent it to her two days ago."

"Really? You never told me."

"I did that intentionally to see what she would think. You know I want you to be happy." Prince said.

Prince and Mattie watched as the two hit it off. It was a wonderful night for James and Antonia. They both chatted about how they felt "destined" to meet – and to be together forever.

James was in his 40's and Antonia, her late 30's, so they were not kids. Both of them felt there was no time to waste. Within a short time, they went on many dates and took numerous trips together. Six months later, James popped the question. He proposed on the Fourth of July at exactly 9 pm just as the first fireworks went off. As people shouted "Ooooo, ahhhhh," Antonia said,

"Oh my God, YES, I will!"

To share the moment, Prince and Mattie showed up to congratulate them at the park.

James, an accountant, had been saving up for the moment when he would find the right lady. He was eager to be a part of the wedding planning, which began right away. Together, they chose the wedding colors, the food, even the bridal gown. James' participation went far beyond the little errands here and there that many grooms do to make it seem like they are part of the wedding.

At the rehearsal, bridesmaids and groomsmen met for the first time, some traveling from out of state to get there. Codie, a good friend of James from childhood, came from Virginia. Codie, who was very handsome, was married with two children and operated his own company in Virginia.

At the rehearsal, Codie and Antonia kept looking at each other. All of a sudden, it clicked. She approached him.

"Did you attend Varsity High in Brooklyn?"

"I did."

"Me too. Oh my God, it's a small world."

"Wow, it *is* a small world," James said, stepping toward them.

Antonia realized that this was the same Codie she had dated for a short time before he moved out of state years ago.

Mattie, who had also gone to the same high school, realized it too. Antonia became very nervous about how James would react if he found out. She excused herself from the rehearsal, taking Mattie with her.

"I'm dead if James finds out. He can be so jealous," she said.

At the same time, Codie tried to compose himself, but he was worried. Did James know he and Antonia had dated? Did it matter? He didn't want the past to affect his friend's wedding -- James looked so happy. Codie figured probably nothing needed to be said because, after all, the relationship was 15 years ago, and James probably already knew all about it.

Mattie, who was staying at a hotel in town, arranged a meeting between Antonia and Codie so they could talk.

"Do we have to say anything to James?" Codie asked.

"Yes, just in case. The only person he listens to is Prince, so we have to let him know about this." Antonia said.

"We can trust him?" Codie asked.

"I think so."

"Why tell anyone? Let's just keep quiet and get through the wedding. In five years, when you have two kids and a solid marriage behind you, then you can mention it!"

"It feels dishonest. Even being here alone with you feels wrong," she said.

"James knows you aren't children – you both have a past," Mattie said.

"Right, of course. There were relationships before we met. Maybe I am being ridiculous, but --" Antonia said.

"We tell Prince, and you'll feel better?" Cody asked.

"He can be the voice of reason if, somehow, James finds out and freaks," Antonia said.

"Let me talk to Prince. I can do it man-to-man. It will seem like a much bigger deal if you try to tell him," Cody said.

Antonia agreed, and Codie promised he'd swear Prince to secrecy.

That night, at the bachelor party, Codie told Prince about the relationship. After an evening of drinking and joking, Prince told James about the relationship. James was stunned. What had been a celebration became a dark night for the groom, who tried to wrap his head around the image of his groomsman sleeping with his bride-to-be. He wondered whether she had hidden this intentionally. His head was spinning. What else didn't he know about her? James confronted Codie,

You never thought to tell me?" he asked.

"I didn't know it was the same Antonia! It was ages ago, Dude!" Codie said. "Really man, its history."

All of his groomsmen tried to reassure James.

"It was 15 years ago!"

"Let the past be the past!"

"As long as you love her, this doesn't change anything. If you love her, marry her."

On the morning of the wedding, the few people who knew weren't sure whether the wedding would go ahead or not.

Late in the day, as Antonia was leaving for her hair appointment, her phone rang.

"James! We aren't supposed to speak before the wedding, Honey!"

"I think you know we need to talk," he said.

Antonia froze, her insides churning. She panicked: furious at both Codie and Prince, terrified of losing James. She said nothing.

"Meet me," James said.

Putting aside custom and superstition, the bride and groom met secretly. She rushed over to him as soon as his car pulled up.

"James, please!" She began to cry.

"It's OK," James said." Unless there is something you have to tell me."

"No, nothing! It was a long time ago. I had forgotten all about it!" she said.

"Is there anything else you aren't telling me?"

"No! Of course not! I would have told you if I'd thought it would matter. It doesn't matter. It was so long ago, long before we even met. We love each other! Please, James."

James' smile was shaky. He knew that with his next words he could make or break her.

"I love you. You are the only one I want," she said.

Even here, with tears in her eyes and fear in her heart, she dazzled him like a diamond. He opened his arms, and she fell into them.

James and Antonia took their vows that day, declaring that from that day forward, they belonged only to each other.

All suspicion has to be suspended, and trust has to be unshakable if you plan a marriage of love and fidelity. If you do not trust the man or woman you are engaged to, get out or get help to forgive and move on. When you jump the broom, carry the bride over the threshold or otherwise make your commitment, leave the past behind, where it belongs.

CHAPTER THREE
CAN'T GET YOU OUT OF MY HEAD (OR BED)

Most of my video clients are in the New York Tri-State area, but sometimes I get referrals from farther away. On the morning I arrived in Maryland to film Tony and Lindsay's wedding, the contact who brokered the deal called me to say that the wedding had been canceled. The chaos that erupted from that announcement prevented him from getting word to me before I left New York. I asked a few questions and found out why the wedding was off. Read below what happened.

Tony had met Lindsay two years previously. Following a whirlwind courtship, he proposed to her, and she accepted. What Tony never mentioned to his fiancée was that he still carried a torch for his ex-girlfriend, Tracey.

Tracey and Tony had split after five years together, but they'd never been able to make a clean break. For two years after the break-up, they were off-and-on. When he met Lindsay they were "off," but Tony was still in touch with Tracey regularly.

On the night of his bachelor party, Tony was a model party-goer. He knew his friends had hired strippers, and he knew that everyone would be drinking. He did not want to lose control and do something stupid, so he limited his alcohol intake, kept his head about him, and refused numerous lap dances. He was happy to report to Lindsey that he was cool and in control whenever she called to check on him.

The party ended at around midnight. The strippers were paid, the room was cleaned, and Tony's boys went to sleep it off in time for the wedding the next day. Tony called Lindsey to tell her the party was over, and he was heading home. Lindsey was spending the night at her parents' house to honor the tradition that the couple should not see each other the night before the wedding. It was rare that they didn't share the same bed. Tony knew he had a window of opportunity.

Tony told his fiancée how much he loved her and that he could not wait to see her at the altar the next day. Then he got into his car, and instead of making a right toward his apartment, he took a left turn and ended up in the parking lot of Tracey's condo. She was expecting him.

Tracey's boyfriend was out-of-town on business, and she and Tony had agreed that he would come over one last time for closure. The last time he'd seen her was five months before, when he and Lindsay had a fight. Tracey had been single at the time. Tony regretted the hook-up afterward, but at the same time, he couldn't believe how much he'd enjoyed it.

Tracey knew so much about him, especially what he liked in bed. As determined as he was to be faithful to his new wife, he hadn't been able to put Tracey out of his head. He told himself this would absolutely be the last time he'd see her.

When he knocked on Tracey's door, she opened it wearing only a bra and panties in his favorite color and style. She took him straight to the bedroom, and they had an amazing night together. Rather than feel sorry, Tony was happy to indulge with Tracey and decided not to feel guilty about anything. This would be the last time, so he made the evening as enjoyable as possible.

As he dozed off, Tony gave Tracey strict instructions to wake him in thirty minutes, which she did. He got up to go home a little while later.

Over at her parents' house, Lindsey was having trouble sleeping. She was excited that in a few hours she would be marrying the man she loved. At exactly 3:17 her cell phone vibrated. Her phone had been ringing off the hook all day and night with last-minute details. She had finally told everyone to leave her alone except for anything really important.

The number that came up was restricted, but Lindsey took the call anyway. A picture was slowly uploading, revealing a naked, sleeping Tony with a woman that Lindsey recognized as his ex-girlfriend. Wearing only a wicked smile, it was obvious that she was holding her cell phone at arm's length for the shocking selfie. Under the image, the text asked,
"Do you know where Tony is right now? He's in my arms and not yours!"

Lindsey's screams brought her parents scrambling to her room. She showed them her phone. Her father immediately called Tony. He answered as he was pulling into his apartment. He had no idea why his soon-to-be father-in-law was screaming at him until he got the forwarded image. There would be no wedding the next day.

Did you notice how Lindsay called Tony throughout the night of his bachelor party? What sneaking suspicions did she have? Was the trust between the two already shaky before the eve of the wedding? Hadn't Tony been lying all along about his feelings for Tracey?

Happy people don't cheat – or, it takes a certain type of unscrupulous person to cheat when they are satisfied at home. All you can do is accept and move on. It is heartbreaking, but if your fiancé's heart is unresolved, better to find out the night before the wedding than a week or a year later. It's harder to get out of a marriage than it is to get in – it's much more than returning gifts and deciding what to do about the catering hall.

The moral of the story: "I do" should never follow "S/He did."

CHAPTER FOUR
DON'T WORRY, I'LL BE FINE!

I remember filming a church wedding for Penny, who was very slim and slight. She looked so frail on her wedding day that I heard the minister gasp when she saw her. Turning to the maid of honor the minister asked if Penny was all right.

"She's been vomiting all day," the maid of honor said.

"Did she eat something bad?"

"Well, we think maybe, but – she also gets nervous sometimes..."

The minister understood how nerves and wedding days are sometimes a bad combination. In this case, there was no need to worry that a local restaurant was ladling out food poisoning. Poor Penny was making herself sick.

Maybe you also have a nervous stomach, and you don't relish the idea of saying your vows in front of so many people. Not everyone likes to be on display. A wedding ceremony puts you in the spotlight in front of friends and family who may have flown in from all parts of the globe to come and see you take this special step in your life. No pressure! What if you slip and fall? What if the wedding starts late or something goes wrong? Scared of your in-laws? Any of these things can cause your stomach to do flips. Or maybe that sick sensation is something deeper; your body's way of saying "stop!"

It's easy for me to say "relax," and it would be meaningless if what you really needed to do was listen to your body's warnings and call the whole thing off. But if you have ruled out regrets, the flu, food poisoning or a hangover, chalk it up to nerves and take stock review your preparations. If you've rehearsed the "thank you" speech a thousand times, practiced your first dance until you know it by heart, you've probably done all you can to prevent a problem. The rest you have to take on faith. There is only so much advance-prep you can do, and only so many things you can control. Do those things and check them off your list.

Unfortunately, illness simply isn't one of the things you can control. So, what do you do if your body acts up on your wedding day? Try taking a few deep breaths if your heart is pounding, and if you are nauseated, try humming. It works. If you feel faint, tell the people around you. Experienced officiants and wedding coordinators know that it's a good idea for a bride or groom to sit down before they fall down. If you feel like hell, it's OK.

Let your armpits sweat, let your nose run. Take whatever cold and cough medicine you need, and be sure someone nearby has a plastic bag for you to use if necessary. It'll be part of the story of your day, just as endearing as that first kiss or that tossed bouquet. Not that tossing your cookies is anywhere near as cute!

The following story is about adventurous Jack, who thankfully, made it to his wedding day to tell me the tale!

Jack loved to try new things. Whether it be exploring new places or trying out new foods, Jack was up for it. He especially loved eating exotic foods from around the globe. The night before his wedding, instead of the typical bachelor party, Jack wanted to go to a new seafood restaurant with his friends. Jack wasn't a big drinker so he wouldn't miss that, and the usual bachelor party just wasn't his thing.

The restaurant boasted an array of seafood, from shellfish to eel. Jack decided he would get a plate full of all different kinds of shellfish. His friends warned him against it.

"What if you have an allergic reaction?" his friend asked.

"What if you get a bad oyster? *That* could keep you up all night and give you a wedding day you'll never forget!" his best man said.

"Don't worry," Jack said, "I'll be fine!"

Jack eagerly ate every nook and cranny of those shellfish. By the time he got home, Jack was beginning to feel dizzy. Since he rarely drank, he figured it was the beers he'd downed and decided that the best thing to do was to get a good night's rest. He was a little annoyed he'd let his friends talk him into having any alcohol at all.

The next morning, Jack woke up sick as a dog with what he first thought was a wicked hangover. After a couple of hours of sipping water and swallowing Advil, he still felt terrible. It dawned on him that this horror could only be a severe allergic reaction to the shellfish. Considering that some allergies can be lethal, Jack realized he was lucky that he had woken up at all.

Jack's face, throat, and tongue were swollen and purplish. He could speak but sounded completely congested, his voice strained. He was nauseated and dizzy. He couldn't remember ever feeling worse. He called his best man in a panic.

"You've gotta come over, man. I'm fragging' sick!" he said.

"What the hell?" Sam said.

"I think I'm having a reaction, this is more than just a hangover, and what if it gets worse? I don't think I can get married today." Jack said.

"OK, hang on, Buddy."

"Can you come over here? I can't drive, and I might need to go to the emergency room."

Sam left immediately to pick him up.

While he waited for Sam to arrive, Jack kicked himself because everyone had warned him against this very thing, but since it'd never happened before, he'd dismissed them. Now he wished he'd listened.

"But I eat seafood all the time. How could this happen?" Jack said to his mother on the phone that morning.

"Honey, you never know," she said.

On his mother's urging, Jack and Sam took off for the emergency clinic where he spent the rest of the morning – canceling all his morning activities and dispatching members of the wedding party to handle the variety of details he was responsible for. From the waiting room, they arranged for tuxes to be picked up and relatives to be grabbed from the airport and train station. While they sat and waited, Jack worried that he wouldn't be at his own wedding.

After a half hour of IV fluids and some Benadryl, Jack was feeling much better, and he was able to assure his bride he'd be at their 4 pm wedding on time. Luckily, by that time, he was feeling much better, though he still looked a little puffy for his photos. Jack made a point to steer clear of everything at the cocktail hour that even sat near the shrimp and clam casino. In fact, Jack swore he was never going to touch another piece of seafood for as long as he lived!

A word to the wise: don't take chances on the day or night before your wedding. If in doubt, stick with the safest choices: a bowl of spaghetti with butter if necessary.

CHAPTER FIVE
HANGOVER

If I had a dollar for every time I heard about wedding-day hangovers, I'd buy you a drink. Frank's story could be almost anybody's. I heard it from the minister who officiated at his wedding. She heard part of it from a guest from out-of-town who was staying at Frank's house. The rest she witnessed for herself.

On the morning of Frank's wedding, he couldn't get out of bed. He writhed as if the daylight scorched him, and he appeared too weak to lift his bowling-ball sized head off the pillow.

"It feels like someone bashed in the side of my head," Frank said. "What day is it?"

Frank ignored his out-of-town guest, who told him it was pretty sad he couldn't remember what day it was, or what we did the night before.

"What, next you'll be asking why you're still wearing the clothes you had on yesterday! What do you think?"

Frank ignored him. After a few minutes of groaning, he got up and looked in the mirror. The bags under his eyes were packed for a three-week trip. He looked like the train he was supposed to get on had run him over instead.

"I'm a train wreck," he said.

Frank was not a big drinker, but he'd made an exception for the night of his bachelor party. Who doesn't? For him, it was the last night to have some fun, so why not celebrate in grand style with his friends?

The men all gathered at a neighborhood bar and started the night off telling jokes and reminiscing about the past. As the laughs continued into the night, so did the booze. One drink after another, Frank drank and laughed – and mixed beers, of course and shots of tequila. Then, toward the end of the night, someone suggested a champagne toast and a move to a nightclub that stayed open later than the local pub.

By the end of the night, Frank was unsteady on his feet and feeling no pain. He had a few teary conversations with his friends, telling them how special they were to him – and everyone got a little sentimental. He turned down food and kept ordering rounds for everyone instead.

"Man, we're supposed to be taking you out, not the other way around!" his friends told him.

"Naw, it's OK, I love you guys!" he kept saying.

Frank's houseguest finally came to his senses, realizing the wedding was in twelve hours. He signaled to the bartender that they needed to close their tab, and he hustled everyone out the door and saw that cabs were called. Being the most sober one there, he put Frank in his car and drove him home, hoping the groom wasn't going to lose it in his new Infiniti.

"I'm not feeling too good," Frank said as they pulled up to his house.

"That's OK Buddy, you're almost home."

His friend helped him up the stairs, showed him to the bathroom, and quickly retreated to the couch downstairs, knowing that Frank was going to have a rough night.

Eventually, Frank fell into bed and slept like a rock. The next morning he woke up with a massive headache, wondering what day it was. When he realized it was eight o'clock on his wedding day, he sat straight upright in bed and started hyperventilating. He had an hour before he was supposed to be at the park for pictures.

As the painful morning wore on, Frank started to wonder about the wisdom of a bachelor party the night before a wedding. Yes, it might be your last night of "freedom" before tying the knot, but maybe, something earlier in the week would have been better? Frank buttoned up his tux shirt praying with all his might that he wouldn't be sick in the middle of his vows.

Frank's critical moment came when he found himself standing at the altar next to the minister. His bride was about to walk down the aisle toward him, and he was swaying on his feet. At first, the minister thought he was just moving closer to get a better look at the bride. Then, she looked at his face and realized he was so pale he was practically glowing. She grabbed his arm as the bride came forward. Carefully guiding Frank toward the bride and her father, the minister whispered,

"Just stay with me, Frank. You OK? Almost there."

No one except the groom could hear her over the swelling sounds of the organ. When the bride's hand was firmly in Frank's, the minister told everyone to sit and instead of bringing the couple up to the altar, she steered them toward the empty first pew.

"Frank and Andrea please be seated."

The bride didn't understand but did as she was told. She stole a glance at Frank and gasped. He looked like he was about to pass out!

The minister handed Frank her glass of water from the pulpit and walked up and down the aisle ad-libbing a homily to take everyone's attention from Frank while he sipped water and composed himself. She joked and told stories, putting the bride at ease, amusing the congregation, and giving Frank the time he needed to recover. When she finally had the couple stand for their vows, the bulk of the wedding was conducted, and there was little more for Frank to do than make it up the aisle in one piece. Frank rallied during the receiving line in the brisk fall air, and only the minister and the bride knew that a disaster had been averted.

Now if you are willing to party like a rock star the night before your wedding, you have to be willing to pay the price the next day. And be aware: if you feel sick and tired, it's going to show in your pictures. The best thing to do is to give yourself at least a day of rest between the bash and the wedding.

CHAPTER SIX
ONE MORE POST AND I'LL UNFRIEND YOU

The best and worst mistakes are always made by the bride and groom. All the other mishaps are just entertainment. These are the ones that echo on down the years. I filmed this rehearsal dinner and heard the rest of the story from the groom months later.

It was obvious to everyone that Tomas longed for his fiancée to pay more attention to him. He had fallen in love quickly and had gotten engaged to Kim within a few months of meeting her. Kim was gorgeous but immature and inexperienced. They committed to waiting until the wedding night to make love – Kim had suggested it. She said it would be romantic, something beautiful to look forward to. Tomas had been touched, and so he agreed. Later, he would come to look at it differently, wondering if Kim had other reasons for putting off his intimate advances.

Kim could be selfish, and she was very concerned about what others thought about her. She seemed to love Tomas but had a short attention span, and so her focus flitted from one thing to the next. He was rarely at the top of the list. When they would go to dinner, she would photograph her food and post it on Instagram. She would take selfies at every date, concert, and beach outing. Even if they stayed home for the evening, there would be a selfie with a comment like,

"Just chill at home."

Tomas wondered if the pictures, tweets and posts were more real to her than the man sitting next to her. Kim was young though, and her family and friends all said she'd grow up and be the bride he dreamed of. He wanted -- with all his heart -- to believe them. When she gave Tomas her full attention, really looked at him, truly loved him when they held each other, his heart soared, and he loved her like he'd never loved anybody before. He prayed that she would outgrow her need to share and compare; please others, flit around social media, and pick up every phone call. He hoped she would change her hyper-connected ways and devote herself to him and (eventually) to their family.

If Tomas had doubts, they got stronger during the months of wedding planning. Kim told her friends every detail. She ran every decision past her sisters, and she brought along her whole entourage to see the venues, florists, and bridal shops. What might have been Tomas and Kim together usually took on a social tone, except when they selected their rings, that she did with him alone. He suspected it was to maximize her ROI.

At the rehearsal, things reached a peak. Calls came in fast and furious, supportive calls and questions, last-minute cancellations, and many congratulations. Kim was on her phone all night, checking in, posting on Facebook. She didn't spend a minute looking into Tomas' eyes but chatted and visited with everyone at the dinner. He watched her, and he wasn't the only one who noticed. Everyone saw that something was wrong. Finally, Tomas took Kim aside.

"Babe, I'm here. I'm trying to get your attention."

But she answered, "Let me just tell them thank you, let me be gracious."

On the night before the wedding, when he should have been excited and feeling more connected than ever to his bride, Tomas withdrew. He spoke to his friends, he even confided in me.

I got a call in the morning. After a restless night, Tomas woke up knowing what he had to do. He called his family, then his friends, to say the wedding was off. He told Kim last.

"You showed me last night how it'll be. You showed me that I will always be last, and everyone is more important than me," he said.

"No! Don't you see? It's just that I was so excited!" she said.

"If you can't share this with me now, how much attention will you give me once we're married?"

He called me right after that to thank me for listening the night before, and to say that my services were no longer needed. The wedding was off. I was glad for both of them.

We all want to be loved and paid attention to. We want to feel that our partner appreciates us and puts us first. In our marriage vows, we promise to "cherish," and that is at the heart of what we all crave.

Maybe this woman was just young and will learn a lesson from the experience, or maybe she will always be this way. We live in such a connected culture that some of us are "virtually" addicted to it. While Kim listened to voice mail and Facebook, Tomas was smart to listen to the uncomfortable feelings inside and not to assume things would get better. He acted on his feelings before he was in an unsatisfying marriage that would have been even harder to get out of. My words of wisdom? It's only too late if you let it be too late.

CHAPTER SEVEN
MOTHER SAYS, "NOT HER!"

You can pick your friends but not your family – and like it or not, that's true of your in-laws, too. You marry the whole clan: the mother-in-law who doesn't like you, the drunk Uncle Bill who shows up at *everything,* invited or not. The brother who is in and out of jail and the children of every former relationship. You are buying in bulk, not an individual package.

A number of brides and grooms find themselves with in-laws who don't approve of them. Most of us hope the relationship will sort itself out over time. But, it may be best to confront the issue before the wedding so your beautiful day won't be ruined by silent treatments, snide remarks, or other displays of disapproval!

If your future in-law doesn't like you, request for a "truce" for the wedding day, or send your partner to lay down the law with their parent.

"Mom, I know you don't like Stacy, but you are not to say a thing to her about her choice of dress, cake, friends, or flowers, got it?"

If you are an idealist with high hopes, call your in-law and invite them to a private talk, just the two of you. Ask the hard questions: "Why do you hate me so much!?" Be prepared to hear the truth, whatever it might be. Once things are on the table, you may be able to talk it out.

If you can't reconcile, come up with some kind of compromise, at least for the wedding day. And remember, a good compromise is one where nobody is completely happy!

Sometimes a bride or groom's parents have a lot to say about their child's choice for a mate. Sometimes it's a cultural thing – arranged marriages depend completely on a parent's choices. But, sometimes, it's just because Mother is a busybody, or Father can't let go of his "little girl." In the following story, Mike's mother has a lot to say because she didn't like his fiancée – but she had good reason. I heard this story through a friend, not through the lens of my video camera.

Mike kept certain facts about his fiancée from his family. He didn't mention that his bride-to-be had three children from two previous relationships. He did not tell them that "Selena" was in the country illegally. He didn't inform them that she was married or how much help she needed; how she didn't even have a home or a bank account when he first met her.

Mike couldn't help himself. Even with all her problems and the red light screaming "NO!" at him, Mike felt like he *had* to help this beautiful, complex woman who was always in trouble. She called him for everything – usually crying or really upset. Before long, he was head over heels in love with her. He was determined to protect her. He decided he would marry Selena so that she could stay in the country. He would give her a home and help her raise her children. He would do anything for her. Mike's friends, who knew much more of this story than his family did, were convinced Mike was crazy and was headed for trouble.

Selena's situation was complicated. Not only was she an illegal immigrant but she was married to a violent man. She wanted to divorce her abusive husband but was terrified of him. He would beat her and mistreat her children. He threatened to turn her in to the INS and refused to move out of the house or to give her a divorce. Selena and the children were forced to leave their home to find a safe place to live and start life over.

Mike became more and more involved with Selena, which his friends thought was just foolish. They warned him that before long the ex-husband would turn his fury on Mike. They were right. There were many confrontations when Mike would throw himself between Selena and her ex-husband. One day, Mike was arrested for assault after stepping in to protect Selena from another vicious beating. It made his blood boil to think of all the years of abuse she endured. When the husband called the police, Mike got thrown in jail. None of his family members knew about it, only his close friends and his pastor.

In spite of it all, Mike proposed to Selena, and she said yes. His friends could not believe that Mike would tie himself to this woman and all her troubles. Mike, Selena, and her three children moved in together in New Jersey. Mike worked at a bank in New York, and Selena stayed home with the kids. It was a rocky relationship from the beginning. He told himself that Selena was a good woman, and all she needed was someone to love her and look after her. Selena must have sensed that Mike was getting cold feet. One day, out of the blue, she told him she was pregnant. Mike was thrilled and even more sure about the relationship.

Mike had no choice but to tell the whole story to his mother and the rest of his family. They told him he was making a terrible mistake, that Selena was nothing but trouble. They said he was crazy to take care of three children who weren't his. His mother even questioned the paternity of the child she was carrying.

Mike and Selena got married in the courthouse and prepared for the birth of their child. It should have been a happy time, but Mike soon found out that his friends and family had been right. Selena wasn't pregnant, and when he figured it out, she cried, telling him she couldn't have any more children because she'd had her tubes tied years ago. Mike was stunned and felt incredibly betrayed. At one time, his family disliked Selena. Now, they all hated her. To them, Mike had been manipulated by a woman who wanted to keep her meal ticket and get her green card. They doubted that she even loved Mike, and they told him this in no uncertain terms.

"She is using you, man."

"Brother, you are out of your mind with this woman."

"Let her go, Mike, she is bad news."

Mike didn't care. He loved her and the children and wanted them to have the American dream of security and prosperity. Mike believed that she had been desperate. She had acted out of self-preservation that was what had made Selena lie to him. After thinking about it, Mike proposed they get married in a traditional wedding, with the white dress and all the rest. Selena jumped at the chance.

The day of the wedding was bright and beautiful. All the plans were coming together without a hitch. As the hour of the wedding ceremony approached, the bride dressed and helped her three children get ready.

At the church, the groom was already standing nervously with his groomsmen, waiting to be called. Mike refused to let anything, even his family's opinion, get in the way of his happiness. The day was bittersweet because many of his loved ones refused to attend the wedding – Mike's mother included.

When she had found out that Selena had lied about being pregnant, Mike's mother knew her intuition about Selena was right. She hoped that if she threatened not to go to the wedding, Mike might call it off, especially since his father had passed away, and he would have no close relatives there with him.

Nothing Mike said had changed his mother's opinion, and time had not worn her down. Mike knew his mother. She did what she said. But, he hoped that on the wedding day, she would not be able to stay away.

When the time came for the honored guests to proceed into the church for the ceremony, there was one person who was conspicuously absent.

"Where is Mike's mother?"

The bride's aunt whispered to her husband.

"I have no idea."

The aunt turned to a cousin in the pew behind her.

"Where is Mike's mother?" she asked.

"Well, I'm not sure I know the whole story…" the cousin said, trailing off as the Wedding March began.

They turned back to face the front of the church to watch as the attendants filed in and took their places at the altar. The bridesmaids were dressed in satin, a shimmering blue that flowed all the way to their toes.

The groomsmen were crisp in very traditional tuxedoes with white shirts and black ties. They stood tall and handsome – each had a posture that said: "I know who I am."

The wedding day went well, everyone enjoyed themselves, and a few family members came to support him. But because his mother wasn't there, Mike couldn't celebrate the way he wanted. And as for the marriage, that was a different story altogether.

Sometimes love is blind and sometimes it sees. It might be possible that people who love you notice something about your fiancé that you can't see. Don't automatically think they are trying to hurt you. They might be trying to save you!

CHAPTER EIGHT
THE BABY'S COMING!

Joyous and stressful moments are inevitable when you're planning a wedding and expecting a bundle of joy at the same time. Between doctor's visits and hair appointments, seating charts and painting the nursery, no one would blame you for going a bit insane. Of course, you wouldn't want your due date too close to your wedding date, but some things are out of our control.

I thought it was sweet that the bride I am about to introduce you to wanted to film her small ceremony. She spoke to me about taping her intimate ceremony as well as the big celebration she planned for later down the road. Recording these milestones for posterity was clearly very dear to her heart.

Ginger was four months pregnant when she started to plan her small wedding. Considering her situation, she thought an intimate ceremony with just a handful of friends and family would be best. She wanted to keep it simple with a toast and some speeches, then finger sandwiches followed by the cutting of the cake. She thought, maybe, after the baby arrived, they would plan a bigger reception with more guests, a menu, and DJ - the whole nine yards. That would be even more wonderful because she could combine the baby's baptism and the wedding reception into one.

For this ceremony, Ginger didn't have a lot of time to plan, but she really wanted to be married before the baby was born and she wanted it to be special – it wasn't enough to go to the justice of the peace with a couple of witnesses. Ginger had to hurry up and get this thing going! She was so frustrated with Jorge because it took a month to convince him to spend the money.

He thought the baby was going to be expensive enough, never mind a wedding, even a small one. After she had convinced him, finally, Ginger only had three and a half months to get everything together. She raced to make a guest list, then picked a generic invitation and got them out over a weekend. She had a hard time finding a caterer who was available on short notice but finally someone came through and even suggested a hall she could rent.

It was pretty basic, so she went online to figure out how to decorate and make it special. She found an officiant, rented plates and glasses, arranged for some music. By her eighth month, with the wedding day coming up fast, she had to settle for some basics, but she was just glad to get to the finish line, get married, and then relax and wait for the baby.

Ginger was exhausted. All the planning took its toll on her. She was sick and tired but was proud of herself for getting everything done in time for the big day. Since Jorge had been against it, she didn't rely on him for many of the details.

Ginger woke up the morning of the wedding starving. She ate a huge breakfast and headed to the salon to get her nails done. Her phone blew up with questions from the caterer, the bartender, and the hall. She forgot to pick up the keys and didn't want to ask anybody to help her. Would she even get it all done?

She finally got off the phone and thought it was safe to take a minute and grab a bite to eat before going to her hair appointment, which took a lot longer than she thought. Finally, she was finished and looked at the clock. She only had about two hours to drive home, get dressed, and get to the church.

On the drive home, she realized she had a headache that she'd been ignoring because of all the details she had to deal with. She took some deep breaths and tried to relax, but halfway home, she started feeling really queasy and lightheaded. She figured it was just stress, but she wished she'd brought Deborah, her maid of honor with her. At least she could have taken the wheel and gotten her back to the house.

No one was home when she finally got there. Being so nauseous slowed her down a lot, but she couldn't help it. Finally, she felt well enough to climb the stairs, to do her makeup, and get into her dress. She was obsessing about the clock – running later by the minute and really getting worried about where her maid of honor was with the bouquets. She grabbed the phone while putting on more mascara.

Ginger suddenly felt a sharp pain. She knew all about false contractions, she'd been having them for weeks. She sat on the bed for a minute to catch her breath. Then, she got up to finish getting dressed. When she turned to leave the bedroom she bent over, caught off-guard by a really strong contraction. Now she was panicked.

No one was home with her – where was everybody? Another contraction. Ginger got downstairs and was looking for the box with her shoes when another pain wracked her body. Why were these contractions happening, and why did they seem to be getting stronger and coming so close together?

"Oh my God, I'm in labor," Ginger said out loud. Ginger didn't want to disappoint her guests. She didn't want Jorge to feel like he had wasted money on this wedding that she had insisted on. She thought that maybe she could make it to the ceremony. The church was only five minutes away, and she was finally dressed and ready.

She reached for the phone and texted Jorge. He called her back.

"Is everyone there at the church?" she asked.

"I'm not at the church yet, honey. Why, what's up?" Jorge said.

"Nothing, no, um, I'm just feeling not so great, you know?"

What, are you kidding?" he asked.

"Well, I think I might be in labor."

"What?! Where are you?"

"I'm home." Ginger bent over double as the pain came again. Breathing hard she came back up."

"Where the hell is everybody?" Jorge yelled.

"I don't know," she said, "Let's just get this going as fast as we can. I want to get married today!"

"I'm twenty minutes away from you. I am going to hang up, call the ambulance, and call you right back. Then I'm on my way to the hospital to meet you." Jorge hung up.

"Wait!" she said. But he was gone. Ginger felt terribly alone. She would be disappointing her guests.

She would waste all the money Jorge was so worried about, because now, it would all be for nothing. She worried about the guests, who had traveled to be there, and she worried that if her water broke now, her wedding dress would be ruined. Not that she could wear in the future anyway, considering how different her figure would look in a few months from now. She slowly climbed the stairs to take the dress off anyway, and in the distance, she could hear the wail of sirens as the ambulance came to round her up. She pulled sweatpants and a tee shirt from the drawer, but before she could get the dress off, her water broke.

The EMT's burst into the house, followed by Ginger's maid of honor, who'd been out picking up the flowers. Deborah was in a panic as she raced in behind the paramedics.

"What's going on? Are you alright, Ginger?" she shouted from the foot of the stairs. She didn't know whether to push past the EMTs or just wait to see what they found upstairs.

When she came round the corner of the bedroom and saw the condition of the dress and Ginger's panting body leaning on the bed, she knew what was happening right away.

"Oh, Ging! It's OK, it's OK, and the baby's coming! It's a good thing!" she said.

Ginger smiled weakly." I'm OK, I just feel bad. And I feel a little sick, too."

The paramedics surrounded Ginger with kind words and instructions to lie back on the gurney. They carried her down the stairs and into the waiting ambulance.

 Now Deborah had to get to the church to tell the guests that the wedding was going to have to be canceled. The good news was the hall was ready, and the food was delivered. Everyone was already in town, and all dressed up, so she invited them all to go over and celebrate the birth of a new baby.

Within just a few hours of the time they were supposed to be married, Ginger and Jorge became the proud parents of Milagra: Miracle. And indeed, she was.

A number of women and men still value the traditional idea of being married before a baby arrives, but western culture has changed, and it is not the stigma that it used to be not to get married, or to walk down the aisle visibly pregnant. Anyway, you know people will talk either way so don't be consumed by what others think.

As most parents will tell you, it's ideal to wait to have babies until after you're finished with school and you have a job and a solid relationship. Anything that can provide security for the baby and opportunity for you will set a firmer foundation for his or her future. However, that little bundle of joy doesn't always come when expected!

Wedding planned or not, prioritize the baby – take care of yourself, and if you must have a ceremony first, don't wait until the eighth month to do it!

Did you notice that Jorge was resistant to the idea of a wedding? Be sure you are on the same page with your partner! Honor each other's concerns about timing and cost, and put the health of mother and baby before everything else.

CHAPTER NINE
WHITE DRESS, GREEN CARD

America! The land of opportunity and promise, where so many people from all over the world come to explore their opportunities and take the chance of living their very own American dream. Even people doing extremely well in their own countries want to see if they can make it here. Just like any place else, the US has its good and bad sides. But, even the negative things don't stop people from all over the world wanting to come to The United States of America.

Yes, they fantasize about the glamour of Hollywood, with the Oscar's star-studded red carpets and the dreams of hitting it big in the movies. They imagine the purple-mountain-majesties and amazing cities, shorelines, and vacation spots. But more than any of that is the great potential of this country. What draws people from all over the globe is the dream that says if you focus and work hard, you will succeed. As an immigrant myself, I strongly relate to Tracey's wish to become a part of this great country.

Tracey came to Miami for vacation from a little town in Spain. She had been to Florida before, but this trip clinched it: she was in love with the city and decided she wasn't ever going home. She was determined to make a life for herself in America.

Tracey knew that there are three things more valuable than gold to an immigrant: A Social Security card, a work authorization, and a driver's license. Without them, you cannot verify your legal status or work, or even enter certain venues, including airports and some public buildings.

There are a few ways to obtain these documents. You can apply to stay in the US if you come in as a celebrity or an athlete. You can come and stay on a work or student visa, or, you can get married to a US citizen.

Tracey was a college graduate, but she had no special skills when she entered the US. She knew she would have to start her life over from scratch, and marrying for a green card was her best option. As the expiration on her visa neared, Tracey became more desperate to find someone to marry. Tracey had always dreamed she would marry for love, and she wondered whether she would learn to love the man she married. Tracey knew it was not an honest way to start a relationship and wondered whether she should let her prospective husbands know about her motives.

Tracey lived with her uncle who worked two jobs and was hardly ever home to counsel her. Tracey decided to take matters into her own hands. She was a beautiful woman, and she used that to her advantage. After her uncle left for work, she would dress up and go to a bar close to the house. She did not go to socialize, but to meet someone to marry – some man who would be the key to living her American Dream. Tracey told herself whatever dishonesty was involved would all be worth it in the end.

After a while, Tracey started dating Peter, a good-looking, successful accountant who was floored by her beauty and instantly smitten with her. She really couldn't have asked for better. Peter was sensitive, he wanted to take care of her, and soon, he fell in love with her.

Tracey found him attractive, and she knew what he had to offer. She had a secret, however, even bigger than her desire for a green card. She was in still love with a boyfriend back home.

Tracey and Raul Skyped all the time when Peter was at work. That wasn't hard because Tracey couldn't work and Peter seemed to work all the time. Sometimes she felt guilty talking to Raul. Sometimes she was furious because Raul was trying to move on. Knowing she didn't want to go back to Spain, he'd been seeing other women. Even though she had moved in with Peter, she didn't feel she was breaking up with Raul. She saw it as making a new life for herself, just like millions of immigrants had done before her. She would do what she had to do. If she could keep Raul in the process, good.

Tracey accepted handsome Peter's ring. She moved into his beautiful home and shared his bed. Her uncle, suspicious, asked her,

"Is this for real?"

Laughing, she answered, "Of course!"

Her uncle had his own struggles to become a citizen, so he closed his eyes and mouth at that point. If she had the stomach for this level of deception, then she deserved whatever happened. Tracey's uncle couldn't pay for any part of her wedding, and her parents back home had no money either. Peter made plenty of money and said he'd happily pay for the hall, the band, rings, and gown – all of it.

Tracey wished that she was able to enjoy her engagement, but she longed for Raul, and Peter was no substitute. She stopped sleeping with Peter, and he got suspicious.

At first, he just thought it was nerves, but his friends said,

"She is using you, man."

"Get a pre-nup. This girl wants to be a citizen and have it all: the house, the fine clothes, and fancy car!"

"That's not true, and anyway, I want her to be a citizen – I want to help her. And, I know she loves me. We're both getting what we want," Peter said.

They set a date. For most brides, a Miami wedding in December would be amazing: nice weather and the holidays coming, but Tracey couldn't get into it. Sometimes she hoped Raul might show up and marry her himself.

In the meantime, Tracey did what she had to do to document her relationship with Peter. She did some research online and found out that it wasn't enough to get married; she had to prove it wasn't a scam. She had to show that they owned things together, that they had bought each other gifts, and they had joint bank accounts. She copied everything, kept notes, and saved it all in a file on the computer, as the websites suggested.

One day, Tracey got a call.

"I know what you're doing, and I don't trust you. I can tell Peter what you are, and if he doesn't sign the Affidavit of Support, you will get kicked out of this country."

"Who is this?" Tracey asked.

"Go through with the wedding. Go ahead. But there are interviews and papers to file. When he finds out about you, he'll refuse to sign the affidavit. You will go to jail."

The caller hung up.

Tracey knew the fine for immigrant marriage fraud was $250,000. She knew marrying just to get a green card could mean five years in jail and deportation. But, people get married for all sorts of reasons, she told herself. How many women marry for security? A good number!

Tracey and Peter's wedding day dawned, cloudy and humid. She was preoccupied as her friends buzzed all around her. Her parents had come from Spain to be with her. All this would be carefully photographed and written in her journal later since the Immigration officers would be looking at the wedding pictures to see if any family had come. It would prove the marriage was not a sham. In Tracey's mind, there was a checklist: buy Peter a wedding present and save the receipt, press a flower he'd given her into the pages of a book along with the card he'd given her, get the pictures taken, sign the new lease together. Check, check, check.

Peter stood at the altar, tall and handsome. Tracey walked nervously toward him, afraid to turn her head to either side, worried that Raul might have come after all and would ruin everything. At the same time, her heart was heavy, wishing it was Raul standing there waiting for her instead of this American accountant with his good hair and nice house.

The wedding was picture perfect, and the reception was beautiful. Everyone had a wonderful time, and no one suspected a thing about Tracey's motives. But, later that night, things changed.

"Who is Raul?" Peter asked.

They were alone together for the first time all day; in the hotel suite they had reserved for the wedding night. Peter was looking at the screen of Tracey's laptop. There was the record of her Skype call from earlier that day. You could see the past few days: all full of calls to and from Raul.

"Raul is a friend. Remember, I told you about him," she said.

"A friend?" Peter was suspicious.

"Why were you Skyping another man –"

"Three times on your wedding day?"

"Well, I – "

"Don't lie to me! What's going on here?"

"Peter – "

It dawned on Peter." My friends were right about you, weren't they? You are using me! You don't love me, do you? Raul? Do you love *him?*"

"Peter, I love you, I – "

"No, don't bother. What a bitch you are – how you used me! Do you have no heart? You went through with all of this!" Peter broke off and grabbing his suitcase, slammed out the door.

Tracey, half in and half out of her wedding dress, collapsed onto the bed. She imagined that turning herself in would be the best thing; maybe she would just be deported that way. She opened the computer again to call Raul.

"Baby. I'm coming home," she wrote in the chat line.

The American Dream is hard to resist, but of course, there are more than broken hearts when fraud is committed. Immigration looks carefully at weddings, they become suspicious when a couple has differences in appearance, age, or religion (and other things as well).

Whether you get caught or not is one thing, but breaking someone's heart is another. Weddings are contracts, economic arrangements, yes. But we file these contracts under the ideals of love, commitment, trust, and fidelity. High ideals -- but that's what this country is built on.

CHAPTER TEN
MARRY ME, TOO!

I heard about this dramatic wedding crisis that happened in a village in the eastern part of Nigeria, among some people from the Igbo tribe. There are several steps to take before getting married according to the Igbo tradition depending on the region where you're from. First, investigative teams are selected from both families to find out about the prospective partner's family background. Second, the families of the bride and groom meet casually, and the groom's family requests the woman's "bride price."

A word about bride price: Long before marriage came to be all about romantic love; it was an economic arrangement between families, tribes, or nations. The Igbo tradition reflects the economics of marriage.

Traditionally, the groom's family brings most of the items on the wedding list, such as a box of fabric, shoes, special drinks, cola nuts, and the bride price. The bride price is for her family because she will leave them and start working and caring for her husband's family. The groom's family compensates her family for its loss. The bride price is also about the expense of raising the bride. They have invested in her, making her the wonderful woman she is.

Now, western ways have been introduced, and everyone wants to do both the traditional and "white wedding" to authenticate their marriage. But, there are customs and rules for how to behave, that's why you rarely hear that somebody is engaged to two people at the same time. No one wants to end up in the hands of a dishonest man!

They had been childhood sweethearts. He grew to be tall and handsome; she, luminous and beautiful. She retained innocence, even into her twenties and after he broke her heart.

He moved to another city to make his way. In his heart, he never truly said goodbye to her. But, he left his home-town, and with that move, he left her behind. There were no words between them. No harshness, but she cried the next few months away until she found her feet again, and she slowly moved on.

After some time had passed, he found himself attracted to another woman. About the same age as he was; lovely and gorgeous. She was from a big, warm family, and she had a great heart. She had no childhood sweetheart, no experience with love before. So when she fell for him, it was hard. He was smitten. In a fairly short time, he asked her to marry him. She said yes.

Work being less than satisfying in this new town, the man returned to the city of his birth where he got a job offer. He told his fiancée that it would only be until the wedding – then they would be together, she would come and live with him in the city of Owerri, and they would make their fortune, join their lives, and build a family.

Returning home meant many things; including revisiting so much of what had been in the past. One day, full of nostalgia for his childhood and all he had left behind, he saw his former sweetheart in the center of town. She was prettily going about her business and didn't see him at first. Assuming they were still on good terms, he stole up behind her and scooped her up into a bear hug.

She squealed, at first in discomfort and fear, but then with delight. Across her face stole a tiny bit of anger and a little bit of sadness as she recalled those months when she cried, those years she spent alone and wondering about him. But she let those emotions go, and she let her words and questions and "I missed you" flow from her heart. They made a date for dinner that night. His innards were on fire, thinking of her the rest of the day. He was eager to be with her, and again, his body longed for her as it always had. He remembered how she felt coming home, like fulfillment and bliss.

Their dinner flew by in moments – they laughed, sharing their memories and everything they had learned and experienced while they were apart. He never mentioned his fiancée. She was far from his mind, a faded picture. Not for a moment did he consider how she would feel betrayed, abandoned. He couldn't allow himself to experience it, and he was utterly captivated by his first love. Nothing else dimmed even the borders of his attention. She was all, she was everything.

He proposed to her that night, offering the contract, filling out the possibilities, letting her decide. She demurred, turning her sweet face away, saying nothing.

As he walked her home later that night, the road was only lit by passing cars, the town blacked-out in a power shortage. She took his hand and smiled tentatively. She wanted to invite him in – but dared not. Even these years later, she was sore, self- protective. Yet, now with the question he had asked her, she sensed she could trust him. This time, she could.

He remained in town for his new work for two months, then six. They saw each other every day, never mentioning the proposal. He never told his first love about his fiancée, far away in another city.

He called the fiancée often, though, while never referring to their wedding. She constantly asked when he would be coming home, and whether she should go on and make plans. Finally, he scheduled a visit with her, one that she anticipated with great joy, and he with some trepidation.

First, he went to see his father to talk to him about his dilemma. Though his father advised him to follow his heart, he was disgusted.

"If someone is beating your drum for you, that is the person you get married to," he said.

He told his son that the woman who becomes his wife becomes an extension of who he is. He said,

"When you see a squirrel dancing on a dirt road by itself, and you see no one around, there is someone beating a drum for him in the bushes. Who is beating your drum? Why are you engaged to two women? This is not how I brought you up."

To his father, this generation was breaking all the rules.

"Now that all this has happened, I won't tell you which woman to get married to. Follow your heart."

The weekend of his visit was difficult but blessedly brief. He broke the news to his former fiancée of his relationship in the city and broke off their engagement. She begged and pleaded and cried. Hysterical, she vowed never to marry. She told him he had ruined her forever –

"Why didn't you just kill me? That would have hurt less than this!"

Her family cursed him out; they got in his face and screamed at him. It was a disaster; beyond anything he could have anticipated. He decided he'd best leave town and not look back. Apologies and amends could be made later. This was not the time.

When he returned home, his sweetheart was eager to see him. Yes, she said. Yes, I want to marry you. And he was transfixed, overjoyed. They immediately made their plans. Her parents, her siblings, her friends, they all said things like; we knew you two would come together again.

Word of the wedding, including the day and time, traveled with friends and cousins back to the city where his former fiancée lived. Every time news came, her heart broke more, and her determination grew deeper. She planned.

The man and his childhood sweetheart went to the priest of their church and did their premarital preparation. They were Catholic and did not follow the customs of their forefathers, but were devoted to the church, which said that one man and one woman join together in Holy Matrimony, a Sacrament. This was as God decreed it – two become one and share their lives in sickness and in health.

Their wedding day approached, and by this time, he barely gave his old girlfriend a thought, but her heart and mind were utterly occupied with thoughts and dreams, and now fantasies, of him. She would make her point, and she would declare her love.

On the day of the wedding, an odd but welcome breeze blew. Everyone stated it was a good sign. It was a blessing for the couple, a fresh start. The church was decorated, the priest was ready, Holy Communion prepared. The guests arrived in fine regalia; everyone was in high spirits for the ceremony and for the reception to follow.

The bride gathered with her attendants at the rear door. By this time, the groom was already in his place at the front of the church, next to the altar, ringed with flowers and the friends of his youth, dressed to stand beside him as groomsmen.

They joked and moved their bodies easily amongst one another, deep, low, rumbling laughter rolling out across the sanctuary as they teased and cajoled the groom, sharing a sort of blood bond: brothers for life.

The music for the procession began. The bride, beaming, stepped into the doorway at the head of the aisle, ready for her slow, beautiful march. But at the side door came a commotion, drawing everyone's attention away from her. She was startled. She blinked and went, once again, to take her first step toward her groom, her future. Again, she was stopped by a ruckus, a disruption, off near the front of the sanctuary at a side door that the priests and altar attendants use to come and go after Mass. What is it? She whispered to her women. They didn't know. But they couldn't send her down the aisle until they did.

Things quieted; the side door was firmly closed.

The ceremony proceeded from the readings to the homily to the vows. Finally, came the question,

"Do you take this woma—?"

The question was interrupted by a woman in a full bridal gown bursting into the room. She had tears streaming down her face. She was followed by her entire family.

The church went wild. People were standing up, shouting, muttering, and talking loudly. The priest lost all control of the room.

The gate-crasher, crying hysterically, "You must marry me as well!"

To the priest, she said, "He is the love of my life! He's got to marry both of us!"

The bride's family went crazy when they heard this.

"What is going on here?" the father of the bride demanded.

The priest held up, and gestured for the woman to come forward.

"Let her come up here," he said.

The bride's family was stunned into silence. Everyone quieted down and took their seats to see what the priest would do.

"What do you want to say, my child?" the priest asked.

"I'm in love with him," she said.

"Love?" Turning to the groom the priest asked, "What do you want to do?"

The priest reminded him that though it might be customary to take two wives in his culture, in the tradition of the Catholic Church it was not done. He told the groom he could go and marry these two, but not here, not today, not in the house of God.

"So, what do you want to do?" he asked the groom.

"I want to apologize to her, but I want to marry the love of my life," the groom said.

The woman broke down, falling to the ground, making a spectacle of herself, screaming and crying. She had to be dragged from the sanctuary with her furious family cursing behind her as they followed her out.

The groom stepped to his fiancée and pleaded for her understanding.

"I am so sorry." He said. This is not what I want. I am as shocked as you are. You are my love, my life, my heart, my darling. Please."

Through tears, she smiled. Maybe someday they would be able to laugh about all this. Not today. The broken heart and dramatic spectacle that had just happened was too raw.

The wedding resumed with the vows, and at the conclusion, the two of them walked hand in hand up the aisle, while their friends and family cheered. He knew there would be some slaps on his back and teasing once they got to the reception. He would accept that along with their congratulations on this most memorable day.

Complicated? Or was the groom simply in the wrong not to break it off with his first fiancée? When it comes to the decision to marry, the best advice anyone will ever give you is to follow your heart. That is, unless your marriage is an arrangement made by family for economic, social, and political reasons. They say that love grows over time in these marriages. I don't know. Maybe *learning* to love, *choosing* to love, and *falling in love* are all possibilities.

CHAPTER 11
MY WEDDING WAS CANCELLED TWICE

I was an award-winning dancer, choreographer, and music video director back in my home country. One newspaper called me "the Spike Lee of Nigeria." I danced with the late Charles Hopst, who was a true champion. I modeled my career after Debbie Allen, a famous American dancer, choreographer, and director. Like many people of my age, I dreamed of going to America to perfect my craft and further myself through education.

Eager for opportunity and at the top of my game, I secured a visa to come to America to participate in a cultural event scheduled to take place in New York. I didn't know what was in store for me, but after the event, I didn't want to go back to the life I was living. I was told that to stay in America, I would have to get a green card. There were two ways I could obtain one: I could marry a citizen, or I could use my talent. Since I didn't want to get married to just anyone, I decided to focus on my career.

I stayed with a friend and his wife and their newborn baby in a one-bedroom apartment. Before long, my friend's wife couldn't take the close quarters, so she asked me to move out. I moved into a church residence, and here is where I met my first wife, a very beautiful, light-skinned, full-figured Black American woman, with a touch of the Caribbean in her blood. She was definitely to my taste at the time.

After just a few dates, I was infatuated with her. I am not sure if it was love. As a Christian, I knew we weren't supposed to have physical contact before marriage, but we did. Two months later, we found out that she was pregnant.

We didn't know what to do and were worried about what people would say: we knew we would be judged by the church, however, here we were. I had to make a decision.

I had always promised myself that if I ever got a woman pregnant, I would do the right thing and marry her, but I had many doubts about marrying her. Looking for help and guidance, we went to the pastor of our church to tell him the news. He was disappointed and said we had no choice but to marry. At this point, I didn't have my clearance for residency yet, so I worked odd jobs, under the table, and had no idea how I would support a baby. The mother of my child was a teacher, but her salary wouldn't be enough. It was a very crazy and unsettled time. The pastor told us not to make too much noise about it, but get married quietly with just a few family and friends in attendance. He made it seem like something shameful that we had to keep hidden. We didn't listen and sent out many invitations in spite of what the minister said.

My fiancée's family was excited. She had four sisters, and she was the youngest and last one to get married. Her mother was very happy that her daughter was marrying an African. Her aunt gave us money to help with the wedding. We set a date and got on the church's calendar. When the news got around the church, people looked at us like we had committed a crime. Church members distanced themselves and people who we considered friends avoided us. We were confused and isolated.

We planned a small wedding of fifty guests. My bride got her dress; everything was ready and paid for: the food, venue, and decorations. My tuxedo was ready for me, and the few friends I had made in America were there to support me. I was ready to get married.

Two days before the wedding, we went to the church for our rehearsal. The church wasn't open, which was the first bad sign. We were told we should come back and do it the next day. That night, I couldn't sleep. I heard a strange voice that night very clearly telling me: *Don't do it!*

I was relatively new to Christ then, and I thought it was the devil trying to discourage me. I started binding the devil and was up till 5 o'clock in the morning. The day before the wedding, my stomach was tight. I had a side gig as a videographer, recording a graduation that afternoon before our rehearsal, which was scheduled for 5 pm. We met with the church secretary that evening and was told that none of the pastors would be available to marry us the next day. We couldn't believe what we were hearing, it was a nightmare. We went home disappointed; my bride-to-be in tears with my baby inside her. This is something you wouldn't wish on anyone.

We started frantically calling people to tell them that the wedding wasn't going to take place, making excuses for the pastors. I almost hated America because of this - I didn't understand how people could be so heartless. We got through the night; my bride went to her sister's house, I stayed at my friend's. If I had an option then, I would have gone back to Africa.

The next day, the people we weren't able to reach were turned away at the church. We didn't go back there for two weeks, and in that time, very few church members reached out to us. Even when we did go back, we felt as if most people were only pretending to sympathize with us. By now, my bride-to-be was three months pregnant. We felt like leaving that church, but something inside me kept saying stay, don't run away from God.

We rescheduled the wedding. This time we kept in close communication with the pastor. We'd planned to have a private wedding ceremony in his office. We kept a very low profile about our wedding: the bride's mother, sisters and my 2 friends would be the only ones to know.

On the morning of the wedding, I called the pastor to confirm he'd be there at 2 pm. We all got ready, and everybody looked good. I called to check in with the pastor at about 1:30 pm. He did not pick up his phone. We sent people to the church to see if he was there, but the premises were locked up. This wasn't funny. The bad feelings I'd been having started up again. By 3 pm, I had left him about ten messages. The bride's mother cried, telling me that no matter what, I *would* marry her daughter that day. I felt my whole life crumbling around me. I was crushed and bitter and angry at the pastor and the entire church. How we were being treated was an outrage. It seemed as if this night was worse than the first.

We decided that we would get married at the courthouse. As Christians, we held on to our faith, and we did return to church and stayed there until my son was born. We didn't run from God but turned to God for strength. It was disgraceful, I just didn't understand it, but my ex - wife and I had to walk in forgiveness and move on.

After some time, I stopped going to the church. I felt as if I was just warming the pew. I didn't get anything from the services anymore. My wife continues to go there to this day. We had a shaky beginning for our marriage. We eventually separated and then got divorced.

What lesson did we learn from this? Those little voices you hear inside when you are about to make a life-changing decision shouldn't be ignored. What if God was canceling the wedding all those times? Maybe, if we had done some premarital counseling with the pastor, it would have helped us. Maybe, he would have known us better and be more faithful to us. Maybe we would have seen that our marriage was not meant to be, or that we would have been able to get past the problems that eventually caused our divorce. We know we did not get the support that we anticipated, but now, we know that people can fail you, but God won't.

All of our mistakes are for a reason: My personal wedding whoops ignited this book idea!

CHAPTER 12
I'VE HAD IT! YOU'RE OUT!

I was there to witness this catastrophe, and the worst part was the disappointment on the bride's face when things went impossibly wrong.

For months, Tanya had carefully planned her reception. She had selected the perfect venue, a beautiful theme, and all the decorations. The lighting and colors were spot-on, and she could not wait for her guests to see the reception hall and to enjoy all of the surprises she had in store for them. The result of all her work was breathtaking. The venue was renowned for its food and the quality of its service – and it was elegantly designed with a stunning staircase leading up to the bridal suite. Everyone who walked into this catering hall was awed by the faux marble columns, the gardens out back, and the luxury suites for the wedding party. The bride and groom had spared no expense for their reception, and I could feel the excitement of the guests.

One of the guests was George, the first cousin of the bride. George looked forward to the reception for one reason: he loved to drink. He didn't care about the finger food that was passed around while everyone waited for the hall to open. For George, cocktail hour was all about the cocktails. He found a seat at the bar and perched there, drinking with his friends and members of the family. George tended to get very loud when he was drinking, but everyone around him was also making noise with glass after glass of vodka, so he didn't seem that out of line.

When the time came to move into the beautifully decorated main hall, the wedding coordinator and the reception staff told the guests to find their place cards and to take their seats. I ran to set myself up to film the entrance of the bride and groom.

Typically, at this point, when everyone moves from the cocktail hour to the main reception, the bar is closed for a brief time. George, who was already tipsy, felt like they were rushing him. At the top of his voice, he shouted out an order to the bartender, who was closing down the cocktail hour. The bartender shook his head, refusing to serve him another drink. Sensing things were about to get interesting, I walked a little closer to film what was going on.

Family members had also noticed, and some came over to George to subdue him before the situation got out of hand. Putting their arms jovially around George, they went to find their seats as the bar was moved inside the reception hall. Everyone exclaimed over the gorgeous flower arrangements, the decorated lighting fixtures, and the hundreds of candles placed around the room. It *was* pretty spectacular.

George was seated at a table with his uncles, nieces, and his mother, who tried to draw him into conversation. Around them everyone was excited, waiting for the bridal party to enter and for Mr. and Mrs. Gilmore to be introduced for the very first time. Waiters came around taking drink orders and bringing out breadbaskets and fresh salads. The guests settled in to enjoy a wonderful night.

Soon, the DJ changed the tempo of the music to get the crowd excited. He called on everyone to get to their feet for the entrance of the wedding party. The bridesmaids and groomsmen danced in as choreographed, all looking beautiful and fresh.

They took their places to welcome the newly wedded couple. Everyone watched expectantly for the bride and groom to come out from the main door to the middle of the dance floor. Even the bridal party was surprised when the couple made an entrance like something out of a movie. The center of the dance floor opened dramatically while smoke filled the room and the pair rose up from the floor into the room. Everyone went crazy, cheering, clapping, and dancing. The couple moved right into their first dance, while the colored lights around the room swirled and changed around them. The excited crowd stepped back to give them room and to take it all in.

Just as soon as the couple finished their dance and everyone was seated, there came a rumble from the bar along with the sound of broken bottles. All eyes turned to see George throw a bottle at the bartender who had earlier declined to serve him. A manager of the venue immediately moved toward George to stop him from throwing anything else. Grasping his arm, everyone could see him lean close to George's ear.

George resisted, pulling his arm away violently and then shoving the manager with all of his strength. Staggering back, the manager's fall was only broken by a guest's chair. Regaining his balance but not his professionalism, the manager threw a shattering punch to George's nose. They both started fighting in earnest. Grunts and fists flew as women, children, and the elderly hurried to move away. I'm afraid at this point I might have lost a few good shots, but people were moving fast, and I had to hustle to protect my equipment.

Lowering my camera, I watched as George's uncles tried to break the two men apart. By this time, however, other employees - coming to their boss's assistance - misunderstood the uncle's intentions.

Instead of helping to quiet the disturbance, relatives and employees began fighting full out. The DJ, realizing that things were not coming back under control, stopped the music, lending an eerie silence to the room, which was only broken by the sound of bodies colliding and falling.

George's drinking buddies from the cocktail hour came around to George's table, seemingly excited to throw themselves into the melee. Some people made for the nearest exits while others shoved tables and chairs aside to try and stop the fighting or get to the injured and bleeding.

The bartender, bleeding from a wound on his head, was tended by two women while wait staff clung to the walls around the room, not sure what to do. Numerous people had cell phones out and were calling 911.

Still standing near the center of the room where they had been dancing, the bride and groom watched in horror as their wedding descended into chaos. The groom looked furious, about to jump on George himself for disrupting his wedding. Only the sight of George's mother crying kept him from doing it. He put his arm around his bride and said a few words to comfort her. I filmed them, but it didn't feel right to barge into their sad moment.

In just moments, the police arrived in response to the 911 calls. The manager met them at the door but didn't try to interfere. He allowed the officers to take control of the room, which they did in short order. As things were beginning to settle down, the manager picked up the microphone from the DJ's table, announced that the evening was over and asked everyone to leave peacefully.

The crowd was stunned. Heads turned from the manager to the bride and groom. Her face registered shock, and then she burst into tears. The groom looked furious, but there was nothing anyone could do.

Many staff members would be going home injured, tables were destroyed, and guests had already disappeared. Neither the coordinator, the photographer, nor I had ever seen anything like it. We couldn't really blame the catering manager for closing the party down. We wondered aloud whether the couple would get their deposit back or if there would be a lawsuit or settlement. I was pretty sure about one thing: It would be many a year before George would be invited to his cousin's house for Thanksgiving dinner.

It is important to know who you are inviting to your wedding day, including family members. You'd be surprised by the number of family members who cause trouble on the wedding day, either because of alcohol, disputes about love-interests, or jealousy. If you know someone who gets out of control after a few shots, you might want to have a chat with them before the big day in order to head off trouble. Worst case: assign somebody to watch over them. Your wedding will be a long-lasting subject of conversation among your family and friends. You might as well have that chatter be positive!

CHAPTER 13
WHO'S GOING TO PAY ME?

The wedding industry has become one of the fastest growing and most expensive in the world. Weddings have gone from simple and traditional to quirky – a drive-by wedding chapel in Vegas – to super-luxurious: an upscale wedding in Dubai.

The rich will order their wedding suit or gown from Paris or Italy and will buy jewels from across the globe. Couples, who can afford it, will fly everyone from LA to Venice to join them for the wedding of their dreams. Meanwhile, many couples will happily keep costs low by getting married in their backyard.

Sometimes couples spend extravagantly on their wedding, forgetting that just down the road there will be credit card payments to make, a house to buy and children to educate. Wedding planning has to go hand in hand with planning for one's future – and the expenses that come along with it. Yes, it is an once-in-a-lifetime celebration, and it's tempting to tell yourself you will worry about what it costs later, maybe asking family for help, or relying on the wedding cash gifts you will receive. Will you be saddling yourself with a burdensome debt? Regret is a terrible way to start a marriage. Be sure the two of you are on the same page, have talked about where the money is coming from, and be clear about a budget. The following story will give you a reason to be sure about that.

Client referrals are the main funnel for my video business. In fact, on average, every client I serve refers me to about five other couples. I was recommended to Joe and Chelsie by a satisfied couple I had worked for.

Joe was in private practice as a neurologist, and Chelsie was a dentist in a hospital. They worked not too far from each other in the city, so they regularly had lunch together – most times Joe bringing food to Chelsie because of her schedule. They were together for about a year and a half before they got married, but they knew they were meant for each other, so they started planning early on.

Both came from wealthy families, and everyone was happy that their children were finally going to get married after some disappointments with previous relationships. The families would share the cost of the wedding. I overheard them saying that the total budget for the wedding was $62,000.

Chelsie was totally in charge of the wedding details. I hardly heard Joe talk at all, except when he was on the phone speaking to somebody.

This wedding was one of the best organized that I have ever shot. Everything was on time. There was one strange thing though: something felt weird about Joe's attitude following the ceremony. He didn't look happy, and since wedding videos are all about the expressions, reactions, and emotions on the faces of the newlyweds, I couldn't help but notice. I had only met with him twice, so I didn't know him well enough to understand why he looked so unhappy. I tried to cheer him up so he would smile for some of my shots.

I usually cut off after the newlyweds give their final word thanks to their guests, and I collect the second installment of my payment before I leave for the night. I get the remaining payment about two weeks later after

I've delivered their video. Sometimes I edit in some honeymoon pictures depending on the package they choose.

Two weeks after Joe and Chelsie's wedding, I called for them to come see the final footage and to check for any corrections before closing out our contract. I left messages for two days with no answer. Finally, after several days, Joe picked up. I greeted him enthusiastically.

"Hey! You know, I want to tell you that you did a great job all through the wedding from beginning to the end," he said.

I had been a little worried when I couldn't reach him, but now I felt some of my concern fade away. But then he continued,

"I have some bad news."

"Really? What's that?" I asked.

"We broke up," he said.

"What? Joe, be serious!"

"I am dead serious," he said." We ended it on our honeymoon."

"After you spent all that money?" I said.

"Yes, after we spent all that money."

I was thinking it was $62,000 spent for nothing. He went on,

"Guess how much we spent for the wedding."

"How much?"

"$86,000 in total," he said.

" My dad was very angry about the whole situation."

"What happened?"

"I guess the best thing I can tell you is that it just wasn't meant to be. Chelsie was having a relationship with someone else. She's with him now, and she's going to have a baby."

"Whoa," I said.

"It's a long story, but I'm moving out West, trying something new," he said.

I sympathized with him, but I didn't know the part he had played in the break-up.

"Um, I'm sorry for your loss?" I said.

"Thanks, don't worry about it, it could have been worse. God knows, it's for the best. Anyway, you've done your job, and you need to be paid."

"Right. OK." I said.

"Our parents signed the contract with you, I guess you'll have to finish it with them," he said.

I sighed and realized I had more work to do before I would get paid. It was sad that Chelsie and Joe had broken up. They had seemed like a great match. I couldn't believe after so much planning, and such an expense, the marriage was over already. I wondered about the emotional toll the break-up must be taking on everyone. At the same time, I had to wonder, was anyone going to pay me my money?

I called Chelsie's parents to ask for the balance. Her father was mad because he put the bulk of his money into the wedding of his first daughter.

"Young man, I am not sure if you've heard the news," he said.

I pretended I hadn't.

"The marriage is over; we will not need the wedding video."

I was conflicted. I felt bad for him, but I needed him to understand that I had done my job, regardless of what happened to the couple. Before I could say anything else, he said,

"Go to the groom's family for your balance."

I tried to get hold of Joe's mother, but her phone was switched off. I went back to Joe

Who told me paying the balance would be a waste of money for him.

Getting no further response from anyone, I gave up trying to collect my fee. I still have the video.

My situation wasn't exactly the same as Joe and Chelsie's, but I understood the expenses, disappointments, and pains of a failed relationship. I am more aware than ever that it's not the amount of money you spend on your wedding that makes it a successful marriage. That requires love, understanding, and being mindful and conscientious of everything happening around you.

As for me, a vendor, I want to remind everyone that the people who work on your wedding day must get paid, even if the wedding reception lasts longer than the marriage itself. You have an obligation to pay, no matter what, even if a contract wasn't signed. Obviously, paying for services rendered is the right thing to do.

CHAPTER 14
FIGHTING ALL THE WAY TO THE ALTAR

Is it a sign of a basic miss-match when a couple fights all the time? Some people are emotionally expressive – they fight passionately, and then walk off arm in arm. Others stay together in spite of real, simmering resentment. How does a couple, a parent, or a wedding guest tell the difference? As the videographer, I can tell if couples are troubled or not after a couple of consultations. The discord between the next couple definitely affected the wedding party psychologically. It was tense as we traveled between the house, the ceremony, and the park, where we took pictures. Both bride and groom were very stiff, I had to make sure they smile and act naturally.

Holly and Ed had been together for so many years that many people assumed they were married. They certainly fought like an old married couple. Some friends hoped that they'd come to their senses and realize that happy couples didn't go at it the way they did.

Around the holidays, Holly and Ed got engaged. They'd been through a period of less fighting, and they were working through some of the resentment and blame that had been their habit. On New Year's Eve, with a ring on Holly's finger, they promised each other they would do better, whatever it might take.

They set a June date and started their wedding planning. Everyone knows how stressful wedding planning can be and how many details are involved. One of Holly's complaints about Ed was his inability to multi-task and his absolute lack of attention to detail. She felt as though she was doing all the heavy lifting with the wedding. Ed acted as if he didn't care. Holly's resolve to be less critical weakened.

Ed loved Holly, but her wild mood swings had taught him over the years that it was best to have no opinion and to go along with whatever she wanted. Some of what she wanted rubbed him the wrong way, though.

First, she was in control of the guest list – and it was big. Since they would be paying for part of the reception, Ed told her that they'd have to cap the list at 200. When Holly reluctantly agreed, she went back to the original list and cut fifty people. Thirty-five of them were Ed's relatives. Second, she insisted on including two of her most catty friends in the wedding party – women who'd ganged up on him numerous times. Whenever they'd had a screaming fight and Holly had slammed out of the door, she had run into their arms. They did not keep it a secret that they despised Ed, considered him thoughtless, spineless, and insensitive. Third, Holly had been reverting back to her former way of talking to him. She was dismissive, disrespectful; and sometimes shut him out of her bedroom.

Family and friends could see there was trouble, and they wondered why Holly and Ed were so determined to get married.

"Holly, it's time for a talk," said her father.

"Daddy, I know what you're going to say. I haven't spent that much money and I know the flowers were – "

He cut her off: "No, it's not about the money. It's about you and Eddie. He's a great guy, but I am not sure you two are a good fit…"

Holly looked at him, confused." How can you say that a month from the wedding?"

"Your Aunt Minnie called your mother. All your cousins are concerned that this marriage will be short-lived."

"We've been together for five years! Why didn't you say something before now?"

"I thought you'd both realize happy couples don't fight night and day," he said.

Her father's words hit home, but at this point, a month out from the wedding, Holly didn't know what to do. Canceling would be embarrassing and expensive with all those non-refundable deposits. Besides, she took it for granted that they'd get married, and the fighting seemed normal to her.

Holly was even more irritated with Ed. Maybe, she was pushing him so that he'd be the one to call it off. Maybe, her doubts couldn't be denied any longer. She got a sick feeling when she thought of the big day.

Holly and Ed made it to the wedding day. They'd had a giant fight at the rehearsal when Ed snapped at Holly for being late, for ignoring him, about frivolous things, such as the wedding presents. Friends and family watched them and shook their heads. It was too late now.

Both bride and groom woke up irritated and impatient. They had both gone to bed angry and unforgiving. Holly's mind whirled, knowing this was not how it was supposed to be, but she pasted a smile on her face and said "I do," to her long-time boyfriend.

Alone in the limousine, their faces sore from smiling for the camera and the crowd, they confronted each other.

"Is this how you're going to be today? If it is, I am not going to put up with it, enough with moods. Get on medication or something. It's our wedding day for God's sake," Ed said.

Holly went ballistic. The driver rolled up the window between the front and rear seats.

"Who the hell do you think you are? You act cold and rude – you ignore me, and I'm the one with the mood disorder?"

They fought all the way to the venue, neither budging. Coldly, they stepped out to greet their friends, not touching, not even side by side. Both dreaded walking out to the hall to receive everyone's congratulations.

The tension was so thick the entire wedding party felt uncomfortable.

"Holly, what's wrong? Come on; put a cheerful face on and sign up for marriage counseling tomorrow! It's your wedding day!" Cherry said.

"I think I've made a big mistake," Holly said.

Ed entered the hall with his groomsmen to hit the bar, leaving Holly and the photographer behind. The camera followed her face and snapped some of the most "real" candid shots of the entire day. Not an hour later, drunk and uninhibited, Ed found Holly with her friends. The guests were nodding in their direction and nervously picking at their food.

"Time for the garter," Ed slurred his words and grinned at her.

"OK," Holly said. The traditions had to go on, after all.

Ed chose his most obnoxious friend, Ralph, to pull the garter down Holly's leg, a tradition that most women would prefer to avoid. They blindfolded Holly so she would think it was the groom.

While the "Stripper" song came on, Ralph pushed up her dress, just to her knees. Holly giggled at first and then gasped. Ralph's hands continued up her legs, between her thighs, and up. Holly stood, ripping off the blindfold and shoving Ralph onto his butt.

"Hey!" he said.

"What the – Ed, you jackass!" she said.

Ed just laughed.

Holly stormed out of the room and didn't return. She had the limo take her and her best friends to the hotel where she and Ed were supposed to spend the night. The next day, she called her attorney for an annulment.

Don't dismiss signs of trouble! Take advice from the people around you who love you and want the best for you. It is never too late to back out, never.

CHAPTER 15
LEFT IN THE LURCH

It is fairly common to hear that a groom or bride "fires" a groomsman or a bridal attendant in the months or weeks leading up to the wedding. Diana let go her alcoholic friend, Yolanda, when her erratic behavior made the bride wonder how she would be at the wedding. Would she cause an embarrassing scene? Would she even show up? Christy fired her cousin, Lauren, when passive-aggressive and outright hostile behavior, including snarky posts on Facebook, made it clear her cousin did not wish her well, but was, rather, seething with jealousy.

These two stories are not about getting "fired," however. Here are tales about unreliable bridal attendants who just don't show up, and how one groom and one bride dealt with the sudden changes right before their wedding days.

Tony went through the roof when his best friend of 14 years called him to say he wasn't coming to the wedding.

"Man, you've got to be kidding me! Why won't you be able to come?" he asked.

"Well, some things have come up." Roger was vague. No matter how much Tony pressed, no answer was good enough. There were complications, too.

First, Roger had the rings. Tony had given them to him the week before at the rehearsal dinner, laughingly saying that he was prone to losing things, and Roger was super-responsible. Roger had stuck the rings in his pocket without a word.

Now Tony wondered if he'd lost them and rather than admit it, was pulling out of the wedding altogether.

"Dude, you still have the rings? What am I supposed to do at a wedding without the rings? Libby will go crazy," Tony said.

"I have the rings," Roger said.

The other complication was that Tony was having a destination wedding – and he'd already flown to Tortuga. It wasn't like he could drive over to his friend's house and pick up the rings. Never mind that nobody was going to fly to Tortuga at the last minute to stand in for Roger.

Tony disconnected the call and paced the hall outside his hotel room. Finally, he strode to his parents' room and told his father that there was a problem.

Richard stepped out and closed the door behind him so that Tony's mother wouldn't hear.

"Did something happen to Libby? To someone?" he asked.

"No, Dad, nothing like that."

"OK, what is it then? You look too grim for a groom on the day before his wedding!"

Tony told his dad that the best man wouldn't be arriving on the island later that afternoon, and in fact, he wouldn't be coming at all. Richard simply asked Tony what he wanted to do.

Tony put his hand on his father's arm and asked him to step in and fill the role of best man. Richard was touched, and he beamed with pride as he walked up the aisle alongside his son.

Though they were without rings, Tony and his bride had their dream wedding, and Tony experienced the nicest gesture a father could offer to his son on his special day. Oh, and the rings arrived at the house a few days later.

Granted, it is rare for an honor attendant to back out so close to the wedding, leaving the bride or groom in the lurch. And, there is no way we can provide for everything that could possibly go wrong when other people are involved.

I'd hope that if you are planning a destination wedding, you have a degree of flexibility and a non-traditional approach, though I have seen how the dream of a destination wedding is even more idealized in a bride and groom's mind. In that case, any variations to their perfect image are even more disruptive. If you are relying on locals to play music, officiate at the wedding, and fulfill your every demand before you arrive at the destination, be realistic. I know a couple for whom the officiant never showed up, and they had to settle for a reception without a ceremony, which they held privately once they were home.

One aspect of Tony's situation would have been easy to fix, and you can take a lesson from him. Keep the rings in your possession until you're about to walk up the aisle.

FROM DENVER WITH LOVE

On the eve of her wedding, Fiona from Denver got a call from her maid of honor, Cassandra, saying that she'd missed her flight. It was snowing like crazy in New York, and there was no way Cassie could get out of LaGuardia airport that evening.

"Fiona, I am so sorry!" Cassandra said, "I've been waiting here for hours, and they are announcing one flight cancellation after the other."

"Could it be they will be shoveled out in the morning, early?" Fiona asked in a small voice.

"I don't know. Honey, it seems like things will be pretty snowed in."

"Oh, OK," Fiona said.

Cassandra would not be at Fiona's "Winter Wonderland" themed wedding through no fault of her own. But she felt guilty. What if she had arranged an earlier flight when she realized bad weather was coming?

"I'm sorry! I feel responsible," she said.

Fiona wasn't upset, as she understood the circumstance. She certainly was disappointed, however, and part of her silence was sadness that her best friend from back home wouldn't be with her the next day.

"It's OK. Really," Fiona said. Then, she took a breath and realized just how upset Cassie was on the other side of the country, snowed in at the airport.

"How are you planning to get home?" she asked.

"Well, they're plowing the streets still. I'll get a cab."

Cassie answered.

"OK, you'd better get going!" Fiona said. Then she added, "Who do you think I should ask to stand in for you?"

"Well, you've always been close to Becky. Why not her?" Cassandra suggested.

"Hmmmm, maybe. I was thinking Rudy would be thrilled to be asked." Rudy was Fiona's 13-year-old sister.

"Ah, Honey, that's a great idea."

Fiona had a beautiful wedding, and Cassandra's absence made Rudy's day very special. Once the wedding was over, and the weather cleared, Cassandra promised a huge makeup luncheon at her house. When that day came, months after the missed wedding, they laughed and cried over pictures and memories of Fiona's wedding day.

There is always a beautiful solution if you look for one. Unfortunately, the highly charged emotion surrounding weddings can blind newlywed to brilliant solutions that will keep the peace and maintain relationships.

Diana stayed friendly with Yolanda, understanding how addiction can turn wonderfully, beloved friends into unreliable and virtually unrecognizable ones. On the other hand, Christy never trusted her cousin Lauren again, in spite of their being thrown together at family occasions. Even when Christy wanted to forgive and move on, the deep jealousy that caused Lauren's bad behavior was still there, and she never forgave her cousin for removing her from the wedding party. Not everyone is able to see the part they play in creating rifts and troubles in their relationships. Better to let someone go than to have to worry what they will say or do on your wedding day. You can mend fences later.

CHAPTER 16
LAST MINUTE

Things can happen beyond our control. The catering hall calls on the morning of the wedding to say that a pipe has burst, and there is no running water. Or the location you chose months ago is not meeting your expectations, and you don't feel comfortable having your reception there. They made many promises to you, but in the weeks leading up to the wedding, they suddenly cannot provide them. What do you do? First, find out if you can get your deposit back! If there is an emergency outside their control, you probably will be reimbursed. It still leaves you in a quandary, though – where in the world will you have your reception?

If you are the one who wants to cancel the contract, consider carefully whether it's worth the price and inconvenience to make this sort of last-minute change. You will lose your deposit, and you might end up spending more money trying to find a new location at the last minute. (Or it might be the best thing you ever did!) You will have the tedious task of calling each of your guests to let them know. Some out-of-towners might need to make alternative travel or hotel arrangements. You will have to call each of your vendors and hope it won't be an issue for them to decorate a different venue (they might see it as starting from square one). The DJ will have to be sure there is adequate power and space for audio and video systems. Is there room enough for the photo booth? Keep in mind there may be additional costs for vendors as well.

In the case of having to change venues on the day of your wedding (we hope not), designate someone to stay at the previous location to let everyone know that there is a problem, and the reception has had to be moved. Maybe a representative from the venue will be kind enough to take on that job. (Along with refunding your deposit, it seems the least they could do if the cancellation is on their end.) You might leave a note with the directions to the new location if all else fails. Your wedding may start a little late, but make the most of it, roll with the punches, and do everything you can to see that your guests get to where they need to be.

In the case of a destination wedding, make sure that the location you have chosen actually exists! If you go online and find the perfect location in another country, make sure you call and speak with a representative first. Never send money overseas for any deposits without talking to someone and confirming your plans. If it is in your budget, take a trip out there and make most of your arrangements before you head back home. The worst thing for you to do is plan a wedding without getting in touch with someone at the location, only to find out on the day that the venue had been closed down months before! As always, get referrals and reviews.

Liane and Will had spent the morning making their last-minute rounds. It was the day before their wedding, and everything was in place. All they had to do now was relax. They were scheduled to be married at sunset at a small lakeside Bed and Breakfast. Everything seemed in order.

That afternoon, as they poured a glass of champagne and started to look at the cards and gifts they received in the mail, the phone rang. Liane answered, assuming it was someone calling to congratulate them.

"Hello!"

"Hello, is this Liane Howell?"

"It is. Who is this?"

"Hi, this is Mrs. Carapace, from Lakeside Bed and Breakfast…"

The caller hesitated, and Liane stood up. She could feel sweat break out on her upper lip.

"Yes, Mrs. Carapace? We spoke yesterday – I thought everything was all set?"

"Well, Liane… Is Will there?"

"Is there something wrong?" Liane was alarmed. She could tell this was not a 'looking forward to tomorrow' sort of call.

When the caller didn't speak, Liane raised her voice.

"What is it? Did your place burn down or something?"

"No," Mrs. Carapace let out a big sigh, and in a rush she said,

"We have had a bit of a problem today."

"What sort of a problem?" Liane asked.

Liane gestured to Will to come over and made a face that told him in no uncertain terms that this was not good. He tried to take the phone from her hand, but she wrestled with him and turned her back.

"What happened?" she asked.

"A guest left the water running in the bathtub on the second floor. They were going to have a bath, as the tub was filling, they fell asleep."

"So one of the guest rooms will be unavailable? I'm sure I can find other accommodations for whoever was going to be in that room!"

Liane was settling down a little. One room out of commission wasn't the end of the world.

"The water ran all night. It came through the downstairs ceiling."

"Into the dining room? Where our reception is? Did you clean it up? Is the ceiling a little stained? I can live with that!" Liane said.

"Actually, the ceiling came down into the dining room. And the water soaked the carpet in there. And, well, there is water everywhere, and the plaster on the ceiling hasn't stopped falling. I'd hoped we could at least salvage your reception, but the damage is too extensive."

"Oh, my God," Liane said.

"You can still have your ceremony out by the lake!"

Liane didn't want to hear another word. She handed the phone to Will and sat down, stunned, her mind going a mile a minute. Mrs. Carapace repeated the story to Will. Grimly he told her he'd call back and hung up.

"She said we could have the ceremony there, and she'd do a champagne toast after, on the porch. She offered to do the cocktail hour outside, too."

"And then what? What about dinner?" Liane asked. "And what if it rains? That porch can't hold fifty people if it rains! OK, everyone can mill around the grounds if it's nice, but –"

"Right," Will said, thinking hard.

"What about our backyard?" Will said.

He sounded tentative, as if he wasn't quite sure. He looked at Liane, doubting that she would take to the idea.

"It's a lot, but we can figure it out with the vendors," he said.

As if she didn't even hear him, Liane grabbed her phone and started googling the wedding venues they had looked at and rejected. It wasn't a big wedding. Maybe someone could accommodate them.

"Maybe a restaurant? Which ones around here have private rooms?" she said.

"Jeez, Liane, really? We wouldn't even have time to go look at anything! What about here, in the yard?"

"But what about chairs and tables?" Liane asked.

"That'll be easier to get than a whole new venue! I'll call Family Rental. They're probably still open."

Liane's shoulders dropped. She sighed.

"Well, do you want to still get married on the lake? I'm a little mad..." she said.

"You can't be mad at the B and B, honey," Will said.

"Call Mrs. Carapace back and find out what it would cost to do a toast and cocktail hour there," Liane said.

Will came back shortly, looking relieved.

"She will do the toast for free, and the cocktail hour at cost. She's really sorry," he said.

"What about the dinner? The cake, the dancing," Liane said, starting to cry. "My God, we are down to half a wedding!"

"Honey, listen. What if we come here after? I'll see what I can rent: tent, seats. If we have the cocktail hour there, it'll give the rental guys more time to set up. We'll get the same caterer that we were going to use. It won't be too big a deal for them to set up here!"

"We don't exactly have a commercial kitchen!" Liane said.

"They manage at-home events all the time. I'll call them too." Will went off to make his calls while Liane went upstairs to find her maid of honor, who'd been staying with them from out-of-town. She told her the whole story but was inconsolable. Will came in to find her distraught.

"Liane, stop! Things happen. We can rent most of what we need and borrow the rest. Let's make a list. I'll call Mrs. Carapace back and tell her we will be there for the ceremony and cocktail hour. Then, we'll make a list, girl! Come on!"

"OK." Liane sounded shaky and uncertain.

Then, her eyes flew open wide.

"What about the guests?" she said.

"We'll call them! Isn't that what the wedding party is for?" Liane's maid of honor said. "And anyone we can't get on the phone, we'll email! Where's your guest list?"

She got to work contacting everyone.

"I'm happy to report that almost everyone took the news in their stride! Looks like they will all still be coming," she said a few hours later.

By 10 o'clock on the wedding eve, whatever could be arranged was arranged. Liane took it upon herself to call the florist, DJ, baker, and caterer, while Will handled the rental agency. Mrs. Carapace assured them that their cocktail hour would be unsurpassed. Best of all, the weather forecast was for sunny skies.

At the end of the day, the lake was glimmering at sunset; all the guests were presented with a tiny printed map to the bride and groom's house. Everyone enjoyed the outdoor cocktail hour, and Liane laughed as her husband toasted her with being the calmest bride under pressure he'd ever seen.

The guests loved the informality of the at-home wedding, and to keep the neighbors happy with the loud sounds of DJ and laughter, Liane had her sister go door to door and invite those folks too. Liane and Will had a wonderful wedding and learned that, under pressure, they can reason together to be a great team.

CHAPTER 17
BETTER LATE THAN NEVER

Ok, so your dress ripped, and you had to rush to find a seamstress. The priest or Rabbi was running late. Your florist got lost delivering your arrangements. Your maid of honor left her favorite lipstick at home and had to get it. There are plenty of reasons for your wedding to start late and none of them are worth breaking a sweat over.

Your guests understand that things happen, but they will appreciate being kept informed. So communicate! Have a close friend or family member let everyone know that you are running behind schedule. Politely ask everyone to sit tight. Consider their comfort. If you're having an outdoor wedding, offer bottles of water to the waiting guests. If the ceremony and reception are at the same location, offer cocktail hour a bit earlier so guests can have a drink and chat -- but don't take so long that everyone is drunk by the time you walk down the aisle!

As soon as I entered the church on that beautiful October day, I saw the bride had chosen to decorate in the shades of fall. Interestingly though, there were no fresh flowers on the altar. Instead, fake Dollar-Store flowers – and a lot of them - in yellow, orange, and brown were scattered all over the floor. A member of the wedding party was taking them out of a plastic bag, pulling the stems off and strewing the artificial flowers around and under the pews. Unlike natural rose petals, these were hard plastic, crunchy underfoot, and awkward to walk on. It was obvious that the church's maintenance man was not happy. It was not going to be easy to clean up.

Half of the wedding party was present, but nobody was presentable. They were using the vestibule of the church as a dressing room. One bosomy woman was trying to tuck the straps of her bra under her armpits (the dress was sleeveless); another was curling her hair. None of the women had shoes on. The groomsmen were un-tucked and untied and didn't seem at all anxious to get themselves together. The three children in the wedding party were completely unsupervised, and while they had arrived nicely dressed, they were looking more rumpled by the minute.

One of the women unpacked what looked like a picnic lunch and called the children over to the balcony stairs where they all sat to eat. No one was acting like attending a wedding that should have started ten minutes ago.

I debated filming this activity, but some of it seemed too personal to record. Instead, I went outside to get a view of the pretty church and perfect blue sky. By 2:30 pm, the wedding was a half an hour late. Only two more bridal attendants had arrived, and not a single guest was in sight. The wedding coordinator, the minister, and the musician were standing in the aisle, drinking Starbucks and talking. I walked over.

"Do we know where the bride is?" I asked.

"No idea!" said the coordinator.

"But we have another wedding at 6, so…"

"OK, I guess we'll just wait?" I said.

"Let me see if one of these women can text the bride and find out where she and all her wedding guests are!" the coordinator said.

"Oh, we're all just on Felicia time!" said the busty woman when the coordinator approached her.

"What does that mean?" the minister asked.

"That she'll get here when she gets here!"

The coordinator looked at me with wide eyes. "I'm not sure what to tell you."

"Well, they have me for the day, so I get paid either way." I sat down to wait.

At a quarter to three, the church was filled with wedding guests. A sunny October afternoon can make a two-hundred-year-old building pretty stuffy. Guests were soon opening windows, unbuttoning jackets, and using their wedding programs as fans.

The heat made people sweaty, and also impatient.

The coordinator, all too identifiable because of the "Wedding Coordinator" badge she wore, had to repeat the same things: "I don't know what's holding up the bride. I don't know when we will begin. No, we don't have a water fountain!"

At 3:15, the wedding was well over an hour late, and the guests, who also had been less than prompt, were getting restless. I overheard a member of the wedding party (by now they were all present except for the bride) say,

"She couldn't pay the limo driver, that's why she's not here."

"What?!" said a wedding guest.

"They wouldn't drive her. I have no idea how she's getting here," said the bridal attendant.

This was news I had to share. When I told the coordinator, she went right to the groom, who'd only arrived fifteen minutes before.

"Listen, we have to have this wedding now! What is going on?"

She said.

"I just sent one of my groomsmen to pick Felicia up. The limousine broke down. It's handled. She should be here in, say, twenty minutes,"

He said.

"Twenty minutes? Where is she coming from?"

The coordinator asked.

"The hotel where the reception is. It's up the expressway,"

The groom said.

The coordinator knew where the reception was. It was more like forty minutes away. "Well, maybe then, we should take care of the rest of the fees, and I'll get the signatures on the marriage license."

I filmed the groom as he produced the paperwork, and the coordinator rounded up two witnesses.

"And, I need to collect the fees for the organist, the sexton, and my fee. And the donation for the church," she said.

The groom pulled out an envelope. "I don't think I have all that, but when Felicia gets here, we'll settle up."

The coordinator smiled politely and turned her back to the groom. To me she said,

"I wouldn't be so sure about you getting paid either today."

At 4 pm, a white Honda Accord pulled into the parking lot. Recognizing the car, the wedding party gathered on the stone steps to watch Felicia get out. The coordinator pushed past all of them.

"Excuse me!" She shouldered her way through the crowd to the bride. "Felicia! Thank God you're here!"

She stopped short as another car pulled in, a Domino's Pizza sign on its roof. Two groomsmen walked toward the car, both counting money as they went.

"What are you doing?" the coordinator asked.

"We ordered pizza."

"Well, you can't eat pizza! This wedding is two hours late and – "she was cut off by the bride who said,

"Can I get a slice? I've been waiting all day, and I'm starving!"

As the bridal party gathered around the hood of a car with two open pizza boxes, the coordinator went inside, fuming.

A moment later the minister came out and said,

"I'm leaving now."

Muttering insults and complaints, the wedding party, trailed by the bride chewing pizza came into the church and finally took their places.

If you are a wedding service provider, collect your fees up front. If you have a sense that anyone is trying to pull a fast one, follow your gut instinct. Do not accept checks. Be clear about time and clean up all the details and expectations you have of your clients. If there are penalties for lateness, spell those out, and do not be afraid to enforce them.

CHAPTER 18
TAKE YOUR TIME

I have spent my share of hours waiting for brides and grooms to get ready, and I make the most of it by shooting candid moments to edit into their wedding video. Caught off-guard by scenes they barely remember always brings a smile. I heard Joy's story from one of her attendants.

Like every bride, Joy wanted to look her absolute best on her wedding day. She had a particular hairstyle in mind and was determined to wear it. Ignoring the advice of her stylist, Joy scheduled her hair appointment for 10 am, which was five hours before her wedding. It seemed more than enough time to Joy. Her hairstylist had tried to schedule a 7 am appointment, but Joy thought it would be too early and stressful.

The stylist always scheduled brides at or before 7 am but she'd given in to Joy against her better judgment. She was more than a bit worried about having enough time, as the hairstyle Joy had requested had lots of intricate details.

"Don't worry, we will have plenty of time," Joy said.

Joy's hair stylist worked her way through her hair, carefully plaiting, curling, and pinning. The clock ticked as the women chatted away, neither realizing the time. Finally, Joy was finished. After viewing her hairdo from every angle in the mirror, she asked the hairdresser to attach the veil with its tiara. Satisfied, Joy turned on her phone and stared at it in alarm. It was 2 o'clock, and the wedding was supposed to begin at 3!

"Marian! It's almost 2 o'clock! Why didn't you tell me?" she said.

"I, um, I told you…um…I wasn't watching the time! I was concentrating!" Marian said.

"Oh my God, what am I going to do?" Joy yanked off the cape she was wearing and ran out the door shouting that she'd pay Marian next week. Before Marian could protest, she was gone.

Speeding toward the hotel where she was getting married and then staying for the wedding night, Joy ran at least two red lights and swore at nearly every driver in her path. Joy was not used to being late – never mind late for her own wedding!

With less than an hour to spare, Joy flung her keys at the valet and raced to her room. Her friends were relieved to see her, and they helped her throw on her dress and slap some makeup on her face. Even with all of this throwing and slapping, Joy was nearly two hours behind schedule.

By the time she got downstairs and taken her place in the procession, the wedding coordinator was seething, the groom was pacing, and the guests were impatient and hungry.

Pasting a smile on her face, Joy walked down the aisle. Inside she was dying of embarrassment because she was raised to be prompt and never to get anyone angry at her. This, for Joy, was the worst possible situation. She was perspiring more than was lady-like and had a dry, pasty taste in her mouth.

When we got to the front of the room, it took every ounce of strength in her not to cry when her angry groom hissed,

"Where the hell have you been?"

Through her smiling teeth, she said, "I'm here now!" She didn't want to admit that the two-hour delay was all because of her hair. She almost wished it was something terrible she could blame it on, like a car accident.

Joy and Ruben were getting married by a friend who had gotten an online ordination just for their ceremony. He made a couple of lame jokes to ease the tension and lighten the mood of the impatient crowd. The bride just nodded and stared straight ahead.

"Just make it short and sweet," she said very quietly. The officiant cut out the two readings – leaving the readers clutching their notes and wondering why they were not called forward -- and deleted his planned, long-winded message. In truth, he was relieved to have permission to cut right to the vows. Immediately after the five-minute ceremony, the couple nearly ran up the aisle.

Smiling now, Ruben asked, "So, what was that all about?"

"Isn't it good luck for the bride to be late on her wedding day?" Joy asked.

"Well, no harm done. And, you look beautiful!"

The moral of this story might simply be to trust the professionals who you are working with. Yes, you will find the bossy photographer and the prima donna hairdresser, but if they say that a hairstyle or a staged photo shoot will take four hours, believe them. If for some reason you wind up unhappy with your vendor, you can always reduce the tip you planned. Though never arbitrarily reduce their stated fee. Settle disputes based on the contract – and be sure you have a contract to rule out any miscommunication!

Finally, take a cue from the groom who, though angry at first, let his frustration go. The focus of the day was joining in marriage with his beloved Joy. That was far more important than the delay.

Telling her she looked beautiful wasn't to reduce the situation to appearance, it was to ease her guilt and lighten her mood. Joy, for her part, is to be commended for letting her embarrassment go so she could enjoy her wedding day. Good for you Joy, that you didn't justify your lateness as some people do, saying "it's my day, and I'll do what I want." Entire Bridezilla seasons were dedicated to this – don't do it!

CHAPTER 19
I HAVE NOTHING TO WEAR!

One of the most important aspects of the wedding is the wedding dress. Many women dream of finding the perfect gown to walk down the aisle in. Whether it is a Cinderella type dress or something simpler, the perfect dress might be the first thing you think about once you get engaged. (Just take a look at any bridal magazine to see the market for wedding dresses!)

A number of things can go wrong with the dress, fit being the most common. First, don't get a dress three sizes too small in the hopes that you will lose enough weight to fit into it on your wedding day. Alterations take more time than you realize. Be careful sizing yourself. Have it done by a professional tailor, seamstress, or staff member at the bridal store. Be especially careful about sizing if you are ordering a dress online. Sizes vary by designer, and if your order is from somewhere outside of your country, keep in mind the difference in sizing. Fabric can affect the fit of the gown, too. Unless your friend or relative is a professional, find someone experienced in wedding gowns to handle any alterations. Do the big fittings a couple of months before the wedding and have a final fitting and pressing two to four weeks before the day.

It is very nice when a mother can hand down her own wedding dress to her daughter. But just remember, depending on how old the dress is, it can be in a very delicate state.

Over time, the color white turns into a pale yellow, especially if it was not stored well. If you plan on wearing your mother's old dress, take it to the dry cleaner and make sure that it can be cleaned and restored without ruining the fabric.

Of course, your dress could tear or get stained. Be sure a bridesmaid has a small sewing kit handy, and bring a bottle of seltzer in the car with you for spills and splashes. Best not to eat or drink in your dress before you head to the ceremony!

This story was told to me by the bride herself while I filmed her getting ready for the wedding.

Mary was excited. Her wedding dress was being hand-made by an Italian fashion designer and would be shipped to her before the wedding date for final alterations. She had carefully researched the designer on the internet to be sure he was reliable, and she had browsed samples of his dresses on his website. One was more beautiful than the next. Once she found the dress she liked, she paid her deposit, and the designer got to work. He promised that her dress would be ready one week before the wedding and that it would be flown "First Class." Mary couldn't wait. She bragged to all her friends and family about the fabulous dress that was being flown all the way from Italy. She even dreamed about it!

The week before the wedding Mary's dress arrived, right on time. She gathered her bridesmaids around, and they opened the box. To Mary's amazement (and relief) the dress looked exactly how she had pictured it. She took it out and spun it around in front of everyone before running upstairs to try it on.

After struggling for a few minutes, Mary had no choice but to admit that the dress was just too small. She was distraught. The dress looked so beautiful; she ached just to look at it, longing to be able to slip it on. She was sure she had given the designer the right measurements. She was confused how this could have happened.

The problem was Mary had sent the designer her measurements 6 months before. She hadn't thought to call or email changes in her size. In fact, she had not been aware that the five or six pounds she didn't lose before the wedding would make such a big difference in the fit of the dress. With only a week to go, Mary had to find a seamstress who could make alterations in time for the wedding. She invested quite a bit more money to get someone who could do the job.

Mary looked beautiful in her dress and only her closest friends knew about the wedding dress drama. I would never have guessed the dress had been an issue had she not told me while I was at her house filming as she prepared for the ceremony.

CHAPTER 20
WHATEVER THE WEATHER

Weather factors into your wedding plans, without a doubt, but who can predict it? Of course, if you dream of a Christmas wedding, a light dusting of snow isn't a disaster. If you pick August, well, plan to sweat.

Keeping up with the weather forecast is iffy, so have a backup plan. For example, if you have your heart set on an outdoor wedding, always make sure that there is a place on site to move indoors. A tent can come in handy if you don't have an indoor facility as back up.

What about destination weddings? It sounds like a lovely idea to have a romantic barefoot wedding by the beach. It's like having the wedding and honeymoon all rolled into one. Jamaica, Mexico, Punta Cana, even Fiji sound wonderful when you are huddled indoors on a cold day in the middle of January doing your wedding planning. But even in the tropics, weather can be an issue.

If you decide to fly your entire family to an island destination for your big day, don't plan to have your wedding during hurricane season. (According to the National Hurricane Center, June 1st to November 30th for the Atlantic and May 15th to November 30th for the Pacific.)

But, once the day is set, the die is cast. Be as flexible as you can with weather-related flight delays and if necessary, bride and groom, you go when the weather seems clear, and if others are delayed, let a few locals be your witnesses. Talk about privacy and romance! Then, when the weather clears and your family and friends can make it, have a nice dinner and share a few informal vows in front of them.

So what happens if you do have an outdoor wedding and no tent, tarp, barn, or other shelter? Here is a cute idea: as a wedding favor, Gina A. from Miami put small umbrellas under her guest's chairs. She originally thought they would be used to block the sun during the midday ceremony. As it turned out, the guests were thrilled to shelter under their umbrellas as a light drizzle fell instead. An excellent idea and a great gift!

Of course, I've filmed during rain showers, but the following story was wet, even by my standards!

Nancy and Chuck were lovers of the outdoors, so it was an easy choice to have their wedding outside. They had in mind a beautiful lakeside ceremony and found the perfect place not too far from home. With all the hustle and bustle of planning, no one had bothered to check the weather report. The drive up to the lake was a beautiful one and setting up posed no problems. There was a small covered area nearby where guests could freshen up in the restroom, but that was it. A few hours before the wedding was to start, the sun slowly disappeared behind the clouds.

"Is it supposed to rain?" Nancy asked Chuck.

Chuck assured her that rain was not predicted. However, Chuck was no weather forecaster, and Nancy's nightmare became a reality. It started raining cats and dogs!

Huddled under the tiny overhang near the bathrooms, Nancy and her bridal attendants wrung their hands as they wrung out their wet dresses. The downpour had begun just as the wedding parties had taken their places under the flowered arch.

Everyone had fled for cover. Most of the guests ran to their cars, where they could be seen tapping away at their phones or chatting animatedly while they wiped dry their fogged-up glasses.

The groom and his party took shelter in the limousine, rolling down the window for a drag of a cigarette or to feel whether the rain was letting up. Their car often seemed to shake as if there was a party inside. Of course, the limo was where the champagne was, and Nancy was sure that Chuck was imbibing. She began to seethe with resentment at her miniscule post under the two-foot awning.

In time, Nancy began getting texts from the guests still hiding out in their cars. Some were ready to head off into town to find a diner for lunch. Others were asking what she planned to do if the weather continued. Frustrated and near tears,

Nancy sent her best woman to the limo to fetch Chuck.

Soaking wet and irritated, Chuck finally arrived at Nancy's side. He took in her smeared mascara and shaking hand, which was still holding a dripping bouquet.

"OK," he said, "so what do you want to do?"

"Is the minister still here?" she asked.

"I think that blue Yugo is her car," he said.

"Go get her, and we can just get married here and be done with it."

"You're the boss," he said, setting off at a jog.

Before long, the two were husband and wife, surrounded by their wedding party and whatever guests were willing to brave the inclement weather under the few umbrellas some people had found in their trunks. At the close of the short ceremony, Nancy's mother asked,

"Now what?"

The picnic tables laden with food and paper plates were soaking wet. Since it was very much a do-it-yourself affair, there was no caterer to call. A few friends not in the wedding party had volunteered to set up and clear away at the end of the reception.

"Let's go into town and see if there's a restaurant that can accommodate all of us," Chuck said. "We'll come back later and clean all this up."

"The Parks Department will love that," said Lucy who was very environmentally conscious. "I'll clean it up and save whatever food I can. How about we go back to someone's house instead? I'm sure there's something out there that's salvageable."

"OK, let's do that," Nancy said, defeated.

"I can call Giuseppe's Pizza and get a tray of ziti, that sort of thing," a groomsman said.

And so it became an 'at-home' wedding, catered by Giuseppe, and patched over by supportive friends who were determined to see that the nature lovers, Chuck and Nancy, learned to appreciate nature in all her forms, including the very wet ones.

It's a very extreme case to be entirely rained out – and to be so unprepared! How could Chuck and Nancy not consider rain? Though I had mentioned the possibility of needing a "Plan B," they brushed it off as it was impossible to rain on their special day. To couples like Nancy and Chuck I have this advice: Be mindful of the 5 P's: PROPER PLANNING PREVENTS POOR PERFORMANCE.

CHAPTER 21
VENUE DISASTER

The reception is the high point of every wedding. Even when guests cannot attend the ceremony, they make sure to get to the party. Every bride and groom hopes and expects it to be perfect, but there are things you can do to ensure satisfaction. First, don't choose a venue that is hours away from the ceremony location, no matter how beautiful it is. No guest wants to spend hours on the road getting there and back, especially if they are tipsy and tired, which isn't fun (or safe).

Next, confirm everything multiple times. Try to step into the venue unexpectedly, or even during other people's weddings. Not to crash, but to peek in and take notes. Most important of all: get referrals from other couples and look into any food safety violations! I shot this story myself, and the whole event stretched out my night much longer than I had anticipated. I felt bad for Burt and Helena, so I hung around throughout and didn't charge extra for my time.

Helena and Burt had chosen their venue six months before their wedding date. Their money was paid, and everything was in order as far as they knew. They had high expectations for their reception.

On the day of the wedding, guest proclaimed Helena and Burt's ceremony the most beautiful they had ever attended. The bride was gorgeous, the bridal party on point, the groomsmen looking sharp in their tuxes, holding cigars, for the photo session.

After the ceremony, as the bridal party took their pictures at the church, calls started coming in from the florist and some of the guests who were already at the venue. There was a reception already going on, and it was in full swing. The coordinator couldn't believe her ears. She left the church in a hurry, dropping everything she was doing to get to the bottom of this situation. Right before she left, she grabbed one of the female attendants and told her what was going on.

"Whatever you do, do not tell the bride! I will sort this out. But, stall!!" she said.

The attendant had no idea what to do to stall the wedding party at the church. The best she could come up with was saying she had to use the lady's room to slow down the picture-taking time.

When the room had been reserved, the coordinator and florist were informed that a wedding would be taking place until 3 pm. After that, they would be able to come in and decorate for Helena's 6 pm reception.

At 3:35 pm the bride and groom occupying the room were only just cutting their cake.

The coordinator went off on the manager. She showed him the contract; she reminded him of the agreement. Most of all, she sweated through her vintage Valentino suit. Where would she put this couple? What was she going to do?

"We were supposed to be in here by 3 pm to set up for Helena and Burt!" she kept saying, spitting in fury. She could see her complaints were not going to accomplish anything. A hundred and fifty people were dancing the Hora and eating wedding cake. They were going to be tough to clear out, even if they were willing and they weren't.

From the look of things, it would be quite a while before this party would be leaving, and then, of course, the room would have to be cleaned. It would take another hour and a half to set up for Helena and Burt, and that would be a rush job. The coordinator wondered about the kitchen. Was the food prepared for Helena and Burt? Were they ready to pass appetizers if she could get her guests into the entry hall?

Just as an inkling of a plan suggested itself to the coordinator, someone from the wedding reception that was underway heard the very heated conversation and ran to tell the bride and groom. They entered the argument, and things got even louder. They offered to pay for another two hours in order to keep the room. The manager didn't seem to know what to do – his reaction was to threaten to cancel Helena and Burt's reception altogether unless the coordinator stopped screaming at him.

By this time, the rest of the guests had arrived and had found out what was happening. They were all gathered outside like an angry mob, giving the management hell. When the bride and groom pulled up in their limo, they weren't sure what they were seeing. Why were all the guests gathered around outside? Was this some fun new ritual to welcome them to their reception? Would they throw rice or release doves or stand in two lines so the couple could walk in past their raised arms? Or, was something wrong?

It wasn't long before the grins of the couple turned to frowns.

"What the hell is going on?" Burt said his lips tight.

"Honey, what's wrong?" Helena asked, peering out the window.

"I'm going to find out." Burt stepped out of the car and approached the crowd, which was all too happy to fill him in. The limo driver became anxious to be on his way.

"You only hired me for four hours. It is not my problem that your catering hall isn't ready."

"You're just going to leave us all here?" The bride asked; her eyes wide. "We don't even know if there's going to be a reception!" She started to cry.

"Hey, it looks like a disaster, but unless I get going, I'm going to have my own crisis on my hands," he said, right before he opened the door for her to get out.

"But – "Helena said, looking lost. She stopped her protest as the limo driver walked swiftly away to get back behind the wheel. Her parents' limo pulled up right behind, just as her car pulled away.

The parents of the newlyweds were furious. The bride's father, who had paid for the reception, was so red in the face that Helena was afraid he would have a heart attack on the spot. She had never seen her dad lose his temper this badly. He was chest-to-chest with the manager, screaming into his face. The police were called.

One level-headed cop took aside the two main players in this drama, the manager and the man who'd paid for the venue: the bride's father.

"OK, gentlemen, how are we going to settle this?" he asked.

"This better be good. There is no settling as far as I'm concerned," said Helena's dad.

"What time is the other wedding over?" the policeman asked.

"They got a late start," the manager said.

"That's not my f----- problem!" screamed the father of the bride.

"Take a breath, please," the cop said.

"They should have been done by 2," the manager said.

"And what time is it now?"

Asked the police officer with mock patience.

"It's almost 4 pm."

"Right. So I am going to walk with you into that room, and we are going to speak quietly to whoever paid that tab and explain that the party's over," the officer said.

"Damn right," said the father.

"And you will give me back half my money!"

"Settle down, we are trying for a solution here," the policeman said.

The men determined they could handle it this way, and the officer and manager went to speak to the bride and groom in the other room.

The father of the bride was considerably calmer when he went back out to the foyer where his daughter was waiting. Sadly, even the bridal suite where she could have gone to cry in private was still occupied by the other bride.

"What's going on, Daddy?" she asked.

"It's all going to be fine, honey."

"Friends," he addressed the people within earshot of him. "There are a few different places around this area: A Starbucks, an Applebee's. Why don't you all get a drink or a coffee and meet us back here in an hour. Everything should be pretty well fixed up by then."

Some people took this recommendation in their stride, while others, including the groom's grandparents, handled it with some complaining.

The bride was bundled back to the church where she and her attendants fixed their makeup, and where the photographer, being a good sport and keeping his cool, took some wedding photos of unusual creativity. He snapped the bride and groom in the cemetery, the bridal party hanging over the altar rail, and the best man and maid of honor pretending to kiss on the altar. It turned out; some of the best pictures of the whole day came from this improvisation.

When the bridal party arrived back at the venue, they saw that the coordinator had made a heroic effort, involving all of her friends and family to set up the room, adding just the right touches where things weren't quite as clean and neat as they might have been. The wedding went on until late in the night, and the story was told for years afterward.

Of course, unforeseen things will occur on your wedding day, but you can prevent major upsets by working with people you trust and getting every detail in writing before you hire anyone or put a deposit down on a hall. Be sure you read the online reviews.

If you have misgivings or if you see that there have been unresolved problems with previous customers, move on, no matter how much you like the venue. Do not trust that your wedding will be the exception.

There are plenty of other choices out there, so do not waste your time, money, and court aggravation. If you have to choose a wedding venue which isn't up to your standards because money is an issue, set your expectations accordingly.

CHAPTER 22
BEST MAN, WORST CASE

"Are you kidding me?"

"You're pulling my leg!"

"Just because I yelled at you last night at the engagement dinner, you're not coming?"

These are just some of the more polite ways to respond to that dreaded phone call. Yes, believe me – it happens; your best man or maid of honor calls you the day of your wedding to tell you that he/she isn't coming. If they are kind, they might call you the day before. Now what?

Usually, the person in this prestigious role is very close to the bride or groom: a best friend or a sibling. Ideally, that special person is there with you from inception: planning, going to appointments, cake testing -- you name it. They even throw you the best bachelor/bachelorette party you could ask for. So, why would they leave you stranded? Well, things happen- serious, unexpected, maybe even catastrophic things beyond anyone's control.

Peter was the groom's best man. They had been friends since high school and right through college. Peter had thrown an amazing bachelor party, keeping the groom safe and protecting him from the guys who would lead him over the line. Peter had been a friend through thick and thin.

On the day of the wedding, I was at the groom's hotel room watching his boys getting ready. Everyone was there except for Peter, the best man, who was nowhere to be found. Members of the entourage called and called his phone, but it kept going directly to voicemail. I could see how frustrated the groom was getting that his best friend was late and would not answer his phone. After a while, the groom looked worried, since this was not like Peter at all.

The limo arrived on time to pick the groomsmen up for the church. Still no one had heard from Peter, including his parents who were also invited guests. They had last seen him as he was going out the door to meet the groom and get ready with the rest of the ushers. As he was leaving, he had said goodbye but didn't mention he'd be stopping off anywhere on the way.

As the time for the ceremony got closer, and all of the men gathered at the church's side door, I saw the groom's frustration turned to full-blown fear. What had happened to his best man? He asked every guest who filed past him. Finally, Peter's parents tapped him on the shoulder. When the groom turned to see them standing there, he knew something was wrong. Peter's parents were in tears when they told him that Peter had been in an accident on his way to the hotel. It was a major accident – Peter had been taken by ambulance to the emergency room.

Peter had a broken leg and was unable to stand. They didn't know the extent of other injuries, and they were rushing off to the hospital. They told the groom that Peter didn't want to ruin his best friend's wedding so hadn't answered any of the frantic calls. It was the doctor who finally convinced him that he should at least call his parents. They could speak to the groom face-to-face.

The groom's first reaction was shock and concern for Peter's well-being. He wanted to go see him in the hospital before the ceremony. He even wondered if he should postpone the wedding, but everyone, including Peter's parents told him "no." Finally, he settled for a phone call before turning to his next concern, which was informing his bride about this change in the wedding line-up. He worried that his soon-to-be-wife's wedding day would be ruined. Everyone told him to leave it alone, so he decided not to call her at all.

The groom smiled to encourage the bride when she walked down the aisle and frowned because she didn't see the best man. She shook her head and appeared to put it out of her mind. But the groom stumbled through the ceremony, clearly upset, though most of the guests didn't know it was because of Peter. At the receiving line, the groom told some people about what had happened, and I heard him mention how much he would miss Peter at the reception – because now, they wouldn't be able to perform the routine they had practiced together for months.

At the wedding reception, the groom took the microphone and finally had the chance to announce what happened to his best friend. As he was finishing his tearful speech, he looked up to see Peter enter the hall in a wheelchair. What had been a bittersweet celebration became one filled with joy, especially watching Peter in his wheelchair dance with the bride, a big smile on his face.

What else can we do but count our blessings when things that we could never expect happen? If your wedding day is impacted by an accident, storm, fire, flood, whatever, don't take it personally! Even on your big day, it's not all about you! Hold the people you love close, and never take them for granted. Find it in your heart to forgive if smaller things prevent your attendant from showing up, and be thankful for everyone who makes it to share the special day with you.

CHAPTER 23
LAZY KATIE

From what I've seen, nearly every wedding party has at least one bridesmaid or groomsman who doesn't take their wedding responsibilities seriously. They are late to everything, don't contribute any money to the parties or gifts, and they skip fittings and rehearsals. They are the "care-free" bridesmaid or groomsman.

Maybe they figure since it's not their wedding, why should they care? To me, being asked to take part in someone's wedding is an honor and one of the sweetest things to experience.

If you have a lackadaisical person in your wedding party, the best thing to do is to sit down and have a talk with them. Tell them how important they are to you; how much you want them to be a part of the wedding festivities – but let them know you mean business!

On the other side of the spectrum, there are the bridesmaids or groomsmen that think it's their wedding. They want to make all the decisions for you or get upset when you don't agree with them.

This is something I think is a special situation, and the bride should be flexible. When it comes to the bridesmaid's dresses, the bride can be a little stubborn. She has a vision and doesn't care what the women in the wedding party think about it. They all want to look their best and sometimes the dress a bride picks doesn't work. She imagines how everybody will look, but doesn't think about all the different body types, heights, and weights of the girls! Brides, listen to your women. If they say they won't be comfortable, then don't make them suffer through the day in a dress that makes them miserable. Consider their opinion, and let them know you appreciate them and all their help and effort.

Most of the time, wedding party drama doesn't impact me, except for the times when people just refuse to be where they are supposed to be for pictures or video. But I do hear stories. All I have to do is comment on the fact that there are an uneven number of women to men in the bridal party, or notice some tension between people. If I ask about it, I get an earful! Once or twice, there have been stories of attendants who got fired at the last minute. Here is Katie's story.

Katie was never on time for any appointments with the bride and even missed the bachelorette party. Jennifer, the bride, dismissed her behavior a few times, but after the 5th missed rehearsal (they were planning a dance number to enter the reception), she'd had enough.

"I'm dropping Katie from the wedding party," the bride told Mary, the matron of honor.

"What? Wow, you've known her for like twenty years," Mary said.

"Yes, but this is so stressful! I can't be reminding and calling and babysitting Katie!" Jennifer said.

"She's been this way her whole life. You can't pretend you're surprised at all."

"I thought, for my wedding, she'd step up."

"Well, she's not going to like it, and neither is her mother!" Mary said.

"Right. Aunt Lana is going to be mad at me."

"Something to think about," Mary said.

Jennifer asked her fiancé to weigh in. He deferred to her because not only was Katie from her side of the family, but he'd never liked her hippie ways and irresponsibility.

Finally, after Katie came to lunch carrying the wrong pair of shoes and insisting they would work much better with her bridesmaid dress, Jennifer had had enough.

"Katie, I am not sure how to tell you this…"

"Tell me what?" Katie looked up mid-chew, like a little kid with ketchup on her lip.

"Katie, I think I have to ask you to step out of the wedding party."

Katie swallowed and looked at Jennifer.

"Seriously?" she asked.

"Yes seriously."

"Why?" Katie looked like she was going to cry, but Jennifer knew that her emotions flew around like a bird in a cage. You could never tell if Katie really felt that bad when she cried.

She just over-reacted to everything.

"Kate! Come on! Do you even know the steps to the entrance dance? Do you know the time of the rehearsal dinner? Did you even notice these shoes are so different from everyone else's? Remember, you did the same thing with the necklace and the hairstyle!" Jennifer said.

"So I'm not going to be a part of the wedding anymore?"

"No. I'm sorry. I'm stressed enough. I don't need a bridesmaid who won't even pick up the phone, won't contribute to the shower, and doesn't even show up for my bachelorette party!"

Katie was devastated, and in the following weeks, tried everything to make up for all the times she wasn't there for Jennifer, but it was just too little too late.

A friend of mine who is a wedding officiant has a theory. She says, "within a year of getting married, every couple will have at least one member of their wedding party they no longer speak to". She believes that most brides and grooms have a gut feeling for who that will be. How can you tell? Well, a groomsman or bridesmaid who is late or inattentive or even passive-aggressive is showing you that the relationship is frayed or there is trouble on the horizon. Maybe the wedding comes at a stressful time for them, or you or your fiancé are being too demanding. Maybe your excitement and joy make the honor attendant jealous or sad. Whatever the reason, do you want a raft of wedding pictures with former-friends in them? It is a drag to explain to your children why someone they have never met stood up for their parents on their most special day.

Sit your friend or relative down, and give them the option of stepping out of the wedding party. You might see such relief on their face – and you might save a precious relationship in the process.

CHAPTER 24
DIDN'T YOU GET MY EMAIL?

Members of the wedding party shared this story with me after the ceremony. Lindsay deserves a lot of credit for keeping it together so well that I didn't realize there had been a last-minute replacement!

Lindsey was the most organized bride around, but the secret to her success and the reason she had everything in order for her wedding was her amazing best friend and maid of honor, Cindy. Cindy was by her side every step of the way, which is why Lindsey was so hurt and confused by what happened on the day of her wedding.

Lindsey hadn't heard a word from Cindy all morning. Her calls went directly to voicemail. As the time came to visit the hairdresser, she just assumed Cindy would show up with a great explanation – and maybe even a wedding present – a little late and apologetic.

When Lindsey got to her appointment at the salon, she found five of her attendants there waiting for her, but no Cindy. They had planned to have their hair styled together, and it wasn't like Cindy to be late. The five other women were angry, but Lindsey was worried. She reasoned that something must have happened to her maid of honor. For hours, she had kept calling while everyone tried to dissuade her. But Lindsay kept saying that it would be just like Cindy to lose track of time while doing something wonderful for someone else. Lindsey had smiled as she tried once more to reach her best woman.

"Cindy?" Lindsey's voice reflected relief, confusion, and a hint of anger when her maid of honor finally answered her phone. "Where are you? It's almost 11! You were supposed to be here by now! Please tell me you are on your way!"

"Didn't you get my email?" Cindy said.

"You're WHAT?"

"I wrote you that I wasn't going to be able to make it to the wedding anytime today."

Lindsey was furious and panic-stricken. "What email? You think I was checking my email on my wedding day?"

"Well, I sent you an email," Cindy said.

"Oh my God! Where are you, and what do you mean you aren't coming to the wedding?" Lindsey asked.

"Look, I'm sorry, but Jack surprised me with a trip to Las Vegas. We are actually on our way to the airport right now!" she said.

"Cindy, how could you do this to me?

I'm getting married in three hours!"

"I, um – "

"That is so tacky!"

"I really am sorry, Lindsey. Please forgive me," Cindy said

But Lindsey was wailing too loudly to hear the apology, however sincere it might have been.

"Try to enjoy your day, OK? I'll make it up to you," Cindy said.

Lindsey's dilemma was on full display for everyone in the salon, including the rest of the bridesmaids. Lillian, who had been friends with Lindsey for years, calmly stepped up to her.

"Linds, it's going to be all right. I'll carry her bouquet; I will stand in for her."

Lindsey had no choice but to agree. The five remaining attendants and the sniffling bride sat down for their hair and makeup.

From my point of view, the day went off without a hitch. I wonder whether Cindy ever made it up to Lindsey, or whether Lindsay gave her much of a chance to. My question is; what kind of person opts for a cheap weekend in Vegas over an once-in-a-lifetime chance to be in her best friend's wedding?

No matter how close they are to you, no single individual should make or break your wedding. Enjoy that special day, and don't let anyone rain on your parade. If there is a serious situation that prevents your honor attendant from being beside you, do what you can to hold them in your thoughts. But if it's an attitude or personality issue, be the magnanimous one - but let conversation and reconciliation be left until you return from your honeymoon!

CHAPTER 25
MONEY OVER MATTER

Weddings can be expensive no matter how small a ceremony you plan. You almost have to go out of your way to get married on the cheap. It somehow turns into a grand affair that you did not anticipate during the planning process. Experiencing a financial dilemma, the day of the wedding can be a nightmare. How can you avoid the situation? The key word is budget! Knowing your limits (and knowing when it's ok to stretch them) is very important, and the bride and groom must be in agreement. Some of us want fireworks and elephants at our wedding, but does it fit into the five-thousand-dollar budget? Probably not.

Once all the hub-bub over the engagement is done, the wedding planning starts. Sit down with your spouse-to-be and come up with a plan. Who is paying for this event? Once you know where the dollars are coming from and you know how much to expect from others, or what you need to save in the next few months or couple of years, you can sit down with a pen and paper and write down a list of things that you would like for your wedding and what they will cost. Research everything so that you know the numbers and can have concrete figures instead of guesstimates. There are the obvious things: the dress, the tux, the venue, and the food. And then there are the extras: the fireworks and elephants. The list can go on and on.

Once you have your budget set and list made, go down the list and decide if they are "must haves" or whether you can leave them off. What's negotiable? What's not up for discussion? Maybe the fancy hotel venue you had in mind is just outside of your means. Could you simplify and only have a cocktail hour instead of a five-hour sit-down or should you choose somewhere more affordable? Having the wedding of your dreams does not always mean you have to break the bank. It just takes a little more creativity.

The day of the wedding is the wrong time to fall short of cash for your caterer or your florist. A screaming match with your wedding coordinator about her final payment isn't a good look in front of your guests, either. Try to make sure that those things are taken care of beforehand so that you don't have to worry about it while you're walking down the aisle.

Another good idea is to create an emergency account, separate from your wedding money. It doesn't have to be a really big amount, just something to dip into if need be.

Lucy and Jack were planning a dream wedding. Jack was the practical type, while Lucy was a dreamer. She was busy cooking up the "wedding of the century." Jack was a little nervous about that idea. Time and again during the selection of venues and decorations, Jack would go the inexpensive route while Lucy went for extravagance: ivory brocade covers for the back of every chair, an ice cream bar and photo booth.

"You only get married once!" I heard Lucy say a few times.

"We hope," Jack replied.

"My God! I had no idea you were so cheap!" Lucy would reply.

"I thought we might be able to buy a house someday," Jack said. "Or afford a honeymoon."

"We'll get wedding gifts, Jack. Susie got like, ten thousand dollars!"

"That wouldn't even cover it," Jack said.

Eventually, after a couple of nights when Jack was sent home to his own apartment when Lucy got frustrated, he got tired of arguing with his fiancé and gave into her lavish desires. In fact, he gave her carte blanche.

"Go for it, do what you want," he said.

Lucy went wild. She chose the biggest banquet hall, with a lobster and steak dinner choice on the menu, and the finest wine. She selected the most beautiful floral decorations you have ever seen. It was going to be a wedding fit for a queen – a royal wedding. She met with me numerous times, to be sure I understood how to video the extravaganza. She chose my most deluxe package with everything included. Some brides buy into the wedding "reality" shows and expect the same for their weddings.

Lucy also went ahead and expanded her guest list well beyond the original hundred people. Jack knew about that part and protested lamely.

"Honey, I know I said you can do whatever you want, but we are talking $85.00 per plate here!"

"I know, but mom and dad really wanted all the relatives invited. Anyway, not everyone will come, and they are helping to pay for the additions anyway!"

"I'll believe *that* when I see it," Jack said.

On the day of the wedding, every one of the 175 guests was impressed from the moment they stepped into the hall.

You could hear them ooh-ing and ahh-ing and murmuring,

"What do you think she paid for *that*?"

"What do you think *that* cost?"

Lucy even included a few things she hadn't mentioned to Jack. A second dress just for the reception, which she justified by saying it was easier to dance in something a little looser. A groom's cake, which she said was her gift to Jack, and a steel-drum band for the cocktail hour. Jack was speechless, and it wasn't a good thing.

The wedding was the talk of the town. What family and friends didn't know was that the young couple was now in a $20,000 credit card debt. Poor Jack had sleepless nights after the grand affair, while Lucy looked through her wedding album reminiscing about her

"Royal wedding."

Lucy's tendencies to spend continued during their first year of marriage. Jack found himself wondering if a divorce would cost nearly as much as his wedding had or if marriage counseling was the more cost-effective way to go. When he finally sat her down to show her their monthly bills and expenses and brought up the idea of a budget, Lucy tearfully agreed.

Sit down together and agree on a guest list and a budget. No surprises. No assuming wedding guests will "cover their plates." If anyone is going to contribute, find out how much and if they are going to put restrictions on what you spend the money on. Get it in writing!

CHAPTER 26
COLD FEET

A friend who is a wedding officiant shared this story from her own personal experience.

Tom and Dana were introduced by friends when Tom was 34 and Dana was 26. Tom had been casually told by his superiors at work that it was time he settled down; that promotions come to employees who have a stable family life and who play by the rules.

She seemed perfect for him, at least at first. He flattered her with his attention. He took her on trips and to fancy restaurants.

He sent magnificent bouquets to her office for no reason except to impress her co-workers.

He proposed only a few short months after they first met. He got off the train late, and they ate a light meal. Then he asked her to come and sit on the couch. He asked,

"I need to know if I ask you this - which you will say yes."

Dana knew he meant that he was about to ask her to marry him. He had been fiddling with something in his pocket all night.

"What is it?" she said. "Of course I will say yes!"

He took a ring box out of his pocket and formally asked, "Will you marry me?"

She felt awkward saying yes. She wanted to stare at the ring, which was everything she hated: a gold band, a marquis cut.

She smiled and said, "Yes," and hugged him so she wouldn't have to look at him. They went to bed and made love, something that had never been a problem for them. The next morning, walking the dog, she told the caretaker of the clubhouse next door,

"I got engaged last night," just to hear herself say it. He politely congratulated her.

Tom wanted to get married soon. They set a date four months away. It almost wasn't enough time to get all the arrangements made.

Over and over in those months, she said "I'm engaged" to herself, waiting to believe it.

Dana thought she was in love with Tom. She loved his big aspirations and generosity, but she sometimes felt that he was arrogant and tried too hard to impress everyone. She hated his mother, and his brother hated her. She thought all of that would work out once they were married.

Tom insisted that she wanted a big princess gown, and a huge wedding party. In truth, she had never dreamed of that sort of wedding. She had imagined something simple, and a classic, simple dress. But, she let herself be convinced. She bought a huge ball gown and invited nine women to be her bridesmaids. The guest list was over three hundred.

The wedding was to be on a Friday evening during the Christmas season, years before that was in style. It would be an elegant night: the women would wear black, velvet dresses in whatever style they wanted and carry brilliant red roses for their bouquets.

Two days before the wedding, Tom told Dana that he wanted her to sign a prenuptial agreement. They had never discussed it before, and she was surprised and affronted. She thought it was a hedge against a divorce, and she could not understand how he could be thinking of that in the week of their wedding. They weren't even married yet, and he was worried they'd get divorced, and she'd get everything. She refused to sign, and after several tense phone conversations, he let it drop.

Dana pressed him that week to find out when they would move in together. Tom had been noncommittal on this point. He had a house in New Jersey, and she owned her own home in New York. He had made no move to invite her, or join her. She assumed, in time that would come, too. After all, their long-distance relationship was one thing. A long-distance marriage just seemed impossible.

On the day of the wedding, Dana took the whole day getting ready, and the girls came to the house at 2 pm to finish dressing.

Her parents came later for pictures, and finally she got into the vintage Rolls Royce they had rented as their limo. It was the coldest day of the year, and a car that old had very little heat. Dana froze in her gown, not wanting to crumple it with any sort of a coat. Fortunately, it was a short ride to the church.

Once Dana and her attendants arrived at the church, she knew something was wrong. The minister had told the groom to get there half an hour before the ceremony, and he was nowhere to be found. Neither he nor his brother was at the church, and as the minutes ticked by, she became more and more certain that she was about to be stood up. Finally, someone came to tell her he had finally arrived. She had always heard it was good luck for a bride to be late, but when it was the groom, it seemed like a terrible omen.

She was escorted into the church and walked down the aisle by her father. The moment she glimpsed the groom she knew that something was wrong after all. Tom had had his hair cut and styled in such a way that he almost looked like someone she didn't know. Who was this guy? What was he trying to say with this new look on his wedding day? They were married by three ministers and a Catholic priest.

The reception ended late, and Tom still didn't seem to want to be alone with his bride. He invited the wedding party to join them in the hotel room where they all hung out, drinking champagne for hours. Finally, after they all left, Tom made a big deal about consummating the marriage. It seemed empty, as if it was his obligation and afterward, Dana stared at herself in the mirror and wondered what she had done.

The next day, they went to Newark to fly to their honeymoon in Bora Bora. It was supposed to be the trip of a lifetime, a honeymoon that anyone would envy. At their stopover in LAX, they got breakfast and a cup of coffee. Just as Dana was taking a bite of her bran muffin, Tom calmly said, "The bars of the cage have clanged shut around me." She never ate another bran muffin.

For the entire trip, Tom didn't once touch his bride. He socialized and made friends during the trip, some he even invited back to New York to visit. The couple never resided in the same house, and when Dana would call Tom to say goodnight, she could sometimes hear a woman's voice. When she asked if he was with someone, he evaded a complete denial saying, "Why would you say that?"

After three frustrating months, during which they saw each other infrequently, Dana saw a lawyer and invited Tom to a meeting at her home saying they had to talk about what was going on. When he got out of his car, a process server met him. Dana heard him say, "Tom Jones?"

When Tom said "yes," the man handed him the papers. It took almost a year for the divorce to become final. Four times the length of the actual marriage. Years later, Tom asked for an annulment on the grounds that it was not a religious ceremony. Dana refused, saying three ministers and a priest had presided, and it was about as religious a service as you could get. Last she knew, Tom had gotten remarried, grown a pot belly, and had a couple of kids. She was glad that he was happy.

Most of the time in these stories you can see that problems come when the couple don't know each other very well and are hurrying to the altar. Sometimes the momentum of a wedding, telling everyone, putting down a lot of money on a venue and other amenities makes it feel impossible to call off. But, the expense of a wedding *plus* a divorce is *a lot!* Save your money, cut your losses, and wish each other well. Then, move on!

CHAPTER 27
LET THE LITTLE CHILDREN COME TO ME

Of course, children can complicate things for a bride and groom. There might be issues of control, jealousy, anger between the child's parent and the soon-to-be step-parent, or the children might dislike the idea of his/her parent remarrying. Every child, in his heart of hearts, wishes for mommy and daddy to stay together. How a couple handles the complications of children from previous relationships is a testament to their maturity, flexibility, and love.

Howard was the twenty-nine-year-old father of two children to whom he was devoted. His first marriage had ended in divorce, and he shared custody of Darrell (5) and Lexie (8) with his ex-wife.
They'd been apart for a year when Howard met Dara and fell head over heels in love with her. He immediately wanted Dara to meet his kids and to be a part of their lives.

"You can't just plop them down into a new family! You'll screw them up." His ex-wife, Casey, said.

"It's not going to screw them up!"

"You can't replace one mommy with another!"

Rather than continue to scream at one another, Howard decided not to introduce the children to his new love for a while. But after a few months, he brought the children to meet her without letting his ex-wife know. What she didn't know couldn't hurt, he reasoned.

He was wrong. When the children (naturally) told their mother all about meeting the pretty, sweet, and kind Dara, who had wanted to impress the children with toys and gifts, Casey was enraged.

"It's bad enough you broke up our family! Now you want to turn them against me and make me the bad parent!" She screamed.

"The kids are fine, and we all have to move on. I am getting remarried, and they have to be a part of our lives," Howard said.

"Remarried? We haven't even been officially divorced for a year!"

The shouting went on, but so did the wedding planning. Dara and Howard decided the children would be in the wedding party, Lexie as flower girl and Darrell as ring bearer.

On the day of the wedding, something was wrong. The children were not ready when Howard went to pick them up. He finally arrived at the hotel over an hour late with two cranky children who still needed to get dressed. He dropped them off with his mother and texted the bride that there would be a delay. His phone rang.

"Howard, we are not going to start this wedding late!"

Dara said. "Honey, it'll be half an hour. My mother's getting them dressed now."

"We are already running late. This is my wedding day!" she said.

"Dara, I—"

"No! Casey did this to ruin my day, and I won't let her. We start on time. If the kids are ready, great, otherwise, they can sit with your mother."

"It means a lot to me to have them up there with us," Howard said, his voice tight.

Dara started to cry.

"I can't believe this," she said.

Just then, Howard's mother stuck her head into the hallway.

"They're just about ready, Howard. I can't do Lexie's hair with the wreath and all, but she looks beautiful anyway."

Relieved, Howard returned to the call.

"We're ready to go Dara. OK?"

"OK." Dara sounded defeated, and that worried Howard a little, but he was thrilled that his children would be standing at the altar with him on his wedding day.

The wedding party looked glorious in their places around the beautifully decorated sanctuary. Howard was proud of his beautiful children and beamed as his lovely bride came down the aisle toward him. What he didn't notice and would have been devastated to see, was his eight–year-old daughter, utterly silent, with tears streaming down her face as she watched her father say "I do" to his new bride.

To avoid issues with the children, every one of the adults must behave like adults, and not like children themselves. If necessary, take the children to a therapist, or talk as clearly and compassionately as you can about your new relationship and the role they will have in it. Reassure them that they are loved above all; remind them that the divorce was not their fault. Gently tell them the decisions you are making. You can get their input, but you are in charge. Don't put the burden of making any choices on them. Be the adult and help them to adjust to the changes that your choices have inflicted on them.

CHAPTER 28
ADULT CHILDREN, BIG BABIES

You would think that the kids most troubled by their parent's remarrying would be the little ones, not the thirty-somethings who moved out of mommy and daddy's house years before. But research shows that grown-up kids take it the hardest of all. According to a New York Times article, when parents divorce, adult children question everything they were raised to believe about marriage and family." It can also cause a significant identity crisis. The trend called the 'grey divorce' is having an impact on grown children that is not clearly understood.

Donna paced nervously in the bridal suite. She was pale and kept biting her lips, taking off her lipstick.

"What's wrong, Donna?" I finally asked. We'd finished with photos and video for now, and I was hoping for some friendly conversation to pass the time and put the bride at ease. Plus, I knew this much stress would show up on her face in her video – which reflects on me. She simply wasn't going to like how she looked in the pictures or video unless she calmed down.

I'm just nervous," Donna said.

"Well, it seems like more than that! And you're getting worse as the time approaches! Are you sure about this wedding, Donna?" I was teasing, but I knew something was seriously wrong.

"I'm sure about Bill," she said.

"Is it standing or speaking up in front of so many people that make you nervous?"

"No…"

"Stage fright?"

Finally, Donna broke down in tears. "What I am really worried about are Bill's children!"

"His children? Are they in the wedding party?" I pulled my notes out of my jacket. I didn't remember children on the list for wedding party photos. I could understand her concern. A kid in a wedding party is always a wild card.

"No, they aren't little children. They are adults -- adults who hate me! That's what I am worried about!" Donna's hand was shaking as she wiped under her eyes.

"Are you worried they won't come? That Bill will be upset?"

"No! I am terrified that they will come and ruin my wedding! I told Bill he could invite them, but I hope to God he didn't!"

Donna told me how she was bombarded with hateful emails from Miles, the eldest son; how she was forced to shut down her Facebook account because of hostile and insulting posts, links to porn sites, and vulgar images. Miles, 36 years old, would leave voice messages – calling her every c-word in the book - until she changed her home number and blocked him on her phone.

"He can't deal with the idea that his parents' marriage wasn't everything he'd cracked it up to be."

She had taken down LinkedIn and changed her email address to avoid his harassment. She effectively disappeared. In the year leading up to her wedding, there were no excited count-down posts on social media, no links to like, no pictures of her engagement ring on Instagram. There were no surprise phone calls from friends who'd fallen out of touch who saw her news on Facebook.

No one could reach her; no one could find her.

Donna handled the isolation and disappointment. She felt sorry for Bill, who seemingly had lost his children when he left Sheila, his ex-wife. But more than anything, Donna was terrified of confrontation by any of these "children" on her wedding day. As a full grown adult, she knew there was nothing she could do to prevent an unbalanced individual from crashing the wedding. She was fairly sure that though she told him to go ahead, that Bill had not invited them or even told them the place or time.

For Donna, finally getting the ceremony over with was a relief. She was married, and on her way to the small reception she and Bill had planned. Sitting beside her, Bill's heart was heavy. In exchange for this new chance at love, he had lost the children he had devoted his life to. At some point, he reasoned, he was allowed to come first. Eventually, they would come around. He wished for that with all his heart. For now, he regretted that his happiness had to come at such a steep price.

It is only coming to light how deeply impacted many adults are by their parents' divorce. With the grey divorce trend on the rise, more and more young and middle-aged adults will face the reality of their parent's separation and possible remarriage. It will call into question their upbringing, their own relationships, and above all, the stability they had assumed while they were growing up.

If mom and dad could divorce after many years together, does that mean they were pretending and unhappy all those years? Did they ever really love each other? What about the lessons they taught their kids about commitment? Here is a niche that therapists and coaches can rush to fill.

CHAPTER 29
MY VOWS

Every religious faith has unique wedding traditions and practices that have been passed down through generations. At the center of the ceremony stand the wedding vows, where we promise to be faithful and loving through good times and bad. It is common these days for couples to write their own vows, or adapt the traditional ones. But, if your ceremony is very traditional – whether Christian, Jewish, Hindu, Muslim, Eastern Orthodox, or another faith – you will have less flexibility in what you can say.

Let's take a quick look at some traditional Christian vows. These will sound familiar, like the ones you hear on TV and in the movies so often.

I, ___, take you, ___, to be my lawful wife/husband,

To have and to hold from this day forward,

For better, for worse,

For richer, for poorer,

In sickness and health,

Till death do us part.

Sometimes "forsaking all others," is in there. It's all pretty much "one and done," no-nonsense, non-negotiable. Do people take their vows seriously? You might think with the divorce rate at (a debatable) 50%, the answer is no. However, marriage rates have *increased* slightly in recent years, and divorce rates have *declined*. I'd like to think that everyone intends to fulfill their vows, whatever the future may hold.

Femi and Sharon were professionals, working in corporate America. They were engaged for two years before they could get their respective families' approval for the wedding.

Both sets of parents were immigrants, though Femi and Sharon were born and raised in the US. They were very attached to their families and respectful of their traditions and opinions. The couple realized their marriage would be uniting their families, so they took their time and hoped that everyone would warm to the idea.

Femi and Sharon were deeply in love and believed in their hearts that only death could part them. Their shared faith was important to them, and they were active workers in their church. Femi was popular amongst the ladies of the church, and some were envious of Sharon for snagging him. At the same time, the beautiful, kind Sharon attracted a great deal of attention as well. Suffice it to say that both were considered "catches."

Sharon was more detailed oriented than Femi, but they both worked a long time on their vows. They were planning to frame them and present them to each other during the ceremony as a symbol of their love. That was unique, and I thought it was cute.

There have been plenty of times when I listened to vows that didn't seem "real;" times when body language and facial expressions just didn't fit the words that were being said. I'd wonder how sincere the bride or groom was; whether they were having second thoughts at that most important moment? Sometimes, one of them seems shocked by the deep sentiment in the vows of the other. Other times, the over-the-top reaction of the congregation, with loud "awwwwws" makes me wonder if they'd never heard personally written vows before!

Femi and Sharon had decided that after they spoke their vows, they would slip them into frames and hand them to one another as a symbol to remember that moment when they pledged their hearts to one another. They had not shared their vows with each other – and because I knew them to be devoted and sincere, I couldn't wait to get to the vows: to see what they would say and to watch the reaction of the congregation.

I had two cameras rolling, one trained on the couple and the other focused on the guests to capture their expressions. As Sharon read her vows to Femi, he was so touched by her words that tears rolled down his face. There were guests who were also moved to tears.

When she finished, Femi didn't go directly into his vows as a groom usually would. Instead, he said,

"Waaaoooo! I'm speechless! Hers are way better than mine!"

The congregation laughed, but when he read his vows to Sharon, they could hear the sincerity in his words. His vows were very different and real. Though very different, both sets of vows were meaningful and truly special, very touching and unique to this couple.

The officiant, my mentor. Dr. Festus Adeyeye then guided them to frame the vows and present them to each other. It was quite moving, and for me, it was a moment that stood out in the ceremony. After the kiss to seal their promises, the bride and groom exited to the cheers and applause of the guests. The beaming smiles on their faces proved to me that they meant every word they said.

I believe that our ceremony is a chance to write our own history, and that is what Femi and Sharon did - something completely unique just for them.

Some couples don't see the vows as a holy moment. They treat it as a formality, a tradition; something that is just a part of the wedding ceremony. I think it is vital to write your promises out, even if you don't want it to be read aloud on your wedding day. It will always be a symbol of your affection for each other, and something to be handed down to your children and your children's children.

CHAPTER 30
MUSIC AND DANCING

Can you imagine the DJ playing the wrong music as the bride starts her walk down the aisle? Or the bride stepping out into the room ready to walk and no music plays at all?

Music is important. It helps to set the mood and also tells a story. From the processional to the recessional, the first dance to the last dance, music has to capture your history: including the first song you danced to or a song that holds a special memory. It has to be softer during dinner and lively for dancing. Music sets the tone and the mood.

Make sure that you meet with your DJ to discuss a playlist for each stage of the wedding. Confirm they have the songs that you request. Ask how many weddings or other events have they played at. Request referrals and look for reviews online. Did others consider your DJ competent and professional? The bride, Joy from Trinidad, was shocked to find that her DJ left the booth and partied the night away with her guests. Nobody had discussed that!

What about live music? If you hire a singer, make sure they can actually sing. Go hear them. And don't ask your cousin to sing because she'll do it for free.

Gladys and Fred were an older couple who hired me to shoot their renewal of vows ceremony. They were excited to be celebrating 50 years of marriage with their friends and family. They planned a small garden ceremony and a reception at a nearby banquet hall.

They had everything arranged except for a DJ. But, what's a reception without music? They asked me for a referral, but my guy was not available. They scanned the yellow pages and found a wedding DJ who fit their modest budget.

The mistake that they made was that they didn't consult with the DJ before their wedding. They didn't check out the DJ's website or supply a list of songs for him to play. Fred did speak to him briefly on the morning of the ceremony and felt confident that he could do the job. Fred assured Gladys that he was a good, affordable choice.

They declined the neon wristbands, the "extras" that the DJ suggested to them.

"Just play some of the old favorites," Fred said.

"Will do," the DJ said.

The ceremony was beautiful, but the reception was another story. The DJ decided that he was going to play the latest songs to hit the airwaves. Clearly, he did not take notice of his older guests. The music was loud and fast, and the guests had favorites from another time. A few people tried to dance, but most sat it out. When Fred suggested that the DJ change the pace of the music, there was not much to choose from. It was a very awkward party to shoot, though some of the footage was pretty amusing.

As the wedding clumped along, Fred approached the DJ to see if he could make some suggestions.

"No Big Bands?" Fred asked.

"Not sure what you mean – these are the biggest bands today!" the DJ replied.

"Sinatra Swing?" Fred asked.

"Nothing like that," the DJ said.

"How about something instrumental then, so we can at least hear ourselves talk?"

"I only have the Wedding March. Do you want to hear that again?" the DJ asked.

"If I came up with an iPod, could you play the music through your sound system?" Fred asked.

The DJ was put out but agreed he could probably do that. Finding a couple of friends with decent playlists, the DJ was graciously invited to sit down and eat something while the groom's son put his parent's favorite music through the speakers.

Simple fix: talk to the vendors before the big day. *Long before.*

CHAPTER 31
ROSES ARE RED, VIOLETS ARE BLUE

You spend hours going back and forth on the phone, sending emails, faxing pictures, stealing flowers from your neighbor's yard, doing whatever it takes to make sure that your florist knows exactly what you want. How frustrating, disappointing, infuriating when they bring you roses instead of violets!

Sometimes, a little common sense would go a long way. We know of a bride who'd ordered her flowers from France. They came in early and were wilted by the time the band kicked up "Here Comes the Bride."

Another bride insisted on out of season flowers in spite of the florist's warnings. Sure enough, those hydrangeas were dead and gray by the time they were set on the altar. But, whether it's the florist or your own insistence on something impractical, by no means should a bad flower day turn into a nightmare for you.

When I met with Melissa to consult on her video package, I was impressed by her enthusiasm for her florist. She told me she had the "ultimate florist." He promised her gorgeous bouquets for herself and the girls, lovely boutonnieres for the guys, huge flower centerpieces for her tables, flower petals on the floor -- the works. Melissa thought that she was having a "Summer Garden" wedding. Boy, was she wrong.

When the newly-married bride walked into her reception hall, she had to blink away tears. Not a single centerpiece looked anything like she had ordered. No grand, sweeping sprays, no robust, blooming peonies. No yellow and celadon-colored roses as she had selected.

Melissa had been thrilled with the bouquets she and the girls carried. They matched her vision perfectly. It had reinforced her confidence in the florist, and though she hadn't seen a sample arrangement like some brides do, she expected to walk into the hall and be amazed. But this was incredibly disappointing -- everything about the centerpieces was wrong. Each table held a small vase, sparsely filled with white lilies. That was it. No greenery, no color, not even a strand of baby's breath to fill out the half-empty vases.

Devastated on the inside but smiling on the outside, Melissa carried on with her wedding as if the flowers were just what she had expected. Melissa's mother watched, proud that her daughter didn't go into a bratty fit. Had she done, she'd be ashamed of herself later, because as it turned out, the florist had broken his leg that very morning, and Melissa's mother had run out to the farmer's market and grabbed whatever flowers she could find.

Later in the evening Melissa grabbed her mother and hissed,

"Do you see these centerpieces?"

"Yes, dear," her mother said.

"I'm fuming!"

"Yes, dear. Look, there's Uncle Mike! Let's go say hello."

Nobody at Melissa's wedding knew the circumstances, and the guests enjoyed themselves, dancing and eating the night away. At the end, everyone complimented her on her fabulous wedding and amazing DJ. Nobody said a word about the flowers. Once Melissa got home that night to pick up her suitcase for the hotel, her mother explained what had happened. Melissa wrote the florist a get-well card as soon as she came home from her honeymoon.

The chances are, your guests won't be paying attention to the things you are so painfully aware of. Don't let them notice what you notice. The more graceful and accepting you are, the more people will know you as someone who *is* gracious and easy-going. The less of a fuss you make; the less attention you call to disappointing flowers, or food, or décor, the more you set an example for everyone that a good time should be had – no matter what. Please don't have a meltdown in front of your guests. It's not worth it.

Sometimes flowers don't make it to the location, or there aren't enough flowers for the bridal party. Melissa's mother had the bright idea to go to the farmer's market where she could get a few flowers at an affordable price. Even your local grocery store has flower arrangements that you can just grab and go. If you find yourself in a pinch, you can avoid flowers altogether and decorate with balloons, fruit, or fabric – or go classic and elegant. Tell the maître d to stash the colored napkins and lay out all the white linens instead. Then, have your sister-in-law run to Wal-Mart for a hundred white votive candles. Put ten or twelve on each table and turn down the lights. Beautiful!

If that's too simple and tasteful for you, nearly everyone has a crafty friend whose eyes would light up at the chance to decorate a catering hall for a bridal emergency!

CHAPTER 32
RING BEARER, RING LOSER

Some brides and grooms are so fond of their nieces and nephews that they will include them in the wedding party, even if the children are too young to walk themselves down the aisle. Children can be adorable, but can definitely add an element of unpredictability!

Stephanie and Andre each had many siblings, and for every brother or sister, there were multiple children ranging in age from 0-15 years old. Every single child, from infant to teen, would be in the wedding party; in fact, the entire entourage would be children. Videotaping children especially when there's a lot of them is a challenge but also fun and unpredictable. I try to be the eyes for everyone, whether they noticed the disruptions and side-shows that go on during the festivities or not!

At Stephanie and Andre's party, the littlest tyke was Milo, who was three months old. They planned that he'd be carried in by his cousin, Tulsa, who was fifteen. Tulsa, being the oldest, was used to shepherding all of her brothers, sisters, and cousins. She was so sure of herself, that at the rehearsal, when little Drew, who was to be the ring bearer, balked at walking down the aisle, Tulsa offered to take Drew in one hand while she held baby Milo in the other. It seemed to work for the rehearsal and the bride and groom thought it was adorable.

Stephanie and Andre imagined being preceded by all of the children, the girls tossing flowers, the boys in white shirts and khaki trousers carrying signs that said things like, "May Love Last a Lifetime."

After all the children entered, Stephanie and Andre would walk in together, hand in hand.

Corralling the children at the church door proved to be a challenge that next morning, but all manner of relatives were called in to assist. The two and three-year-olds took their sweet time getting down the aisle with their signs and flowers, but they were coaxed by their parents who were strategically placed at the front of the church and in the pews mid-way down the aisle. Roger, who was four, saw a friend in the congregation, and he paused to wave but quickly remembered himself. Little Becca, only 2 years old, became frightened at the "Awwwwww" everyone said when they saw her, and she sat down on the carpet to cry.

Finally, it was Tulsa's turn. Her hands were full with Milo the baby and with Drew, the ring bearer. Drew swung the pillow to and fro, on which the rings were firmly tied. From time to time, he would look down at it and try to vigorously shake the rings off.

Fortunately, they stayed in place.

Tulsa stood erect and proud, jostling the baby higher up on her hip; she pasted a smile on her face and took her first step into the sanctuary. Little Drew remained wedged in the door. He was suddenly shy. Tulsa whispered through her teeth,

"Drew, not now! Come on!"

"Naaaawwwwwww!" said Drew.

"Drew, please!" The baby Milo found a long corkscrew curl on Tulsa's head and yanked. She made a face. The pain distracted Tulsa for a moment, and a tiny bit of her confidence slipped. Tulsa was slim and slight, and carrying the pudgy Milo was a challenge. He was at least twice the size of a normal three-month-old. Weighed down with squirmy baby Milo on one side and pulled and tugged by stubborn Drew on the other, Tulsa's lovely yellow dress was becoming wrinkled, her hair was coming undone, and her patience was ebbing away. All of this was obvious to everyone watching.

The bride and groom were blissfully unaware of the struggle their niece was having. They were still in the vestibule, waiting for the signal that it was time for them to make their entrance.

Finally, the inevitable happened: Drew broke free. With whoops of liberation, Drew threw himself down the aisle, banging the pillow against his hip the way a cowboy would flog his horse with his hat. Tulsa grimly followed Drew up the aisle, and giving up her guardianship of the boy, she took her place at the altar.

Drew was finally corralled by his mother and perched on her lap. Here he would stay until the time came for him to fulfill his role as super ring bearer.

Stephanie and Andre came in, casual and hip; their outfits echoing themes. The children wore: khaki, white cotton, rustic-looking flowers. They turned to each other, and the minister began,

"Dearly beloved…"

Of course, the ceremony was somewhat interrupted by the sounds of the many children, but since nearly everyone present was related to them in some way, no one cared.

When it came time for the rings to be exchanged, Drew's mother set him on his feet and gently shoved him in the general direction of the bride and groom.

"Go give Andre Aunt Stephie's ring, Baby," she said.

Drew strode deliberately, his chest puffed out, toward his aunt, swinging the ring pillow at his side. As he got to her, he thrust the pillow at her and said,

"Here!"

Stephanie reached for the pillow as Drew let it go, and it fell to the floor. Laughing, everyone watched as the bride bent to pick it up. Drew returned to his mother and started to tell her all about his long walk to the bride. Everybody could hear him say,

"See Mommy! I did it!"

The bride stood up, looked at the pillow, gasped.

The rings were gone.

"Where are the rings?" she said.

Andre knelt to search. Stephanie looked at her sister.

"Do you have them?" she mouthed. "Does Drew have them?"

The guests sitting in the front rows started to look around their feet for the rings. The way the boy had been swinging the pillow meant that those two symbols of wedded bliss could be anywhere in the room. The children at the altar, all sensing a more free-flowing mood taking over, started to prattle and move out of the orbits they'd been stationed in. People muttered about what bad luck this was, to lose the wedding rings; what a sign of pending doom for the couple.

The rings were eventually found by the cleaning staff later that week and returned in due time to the rightful owners. For the ceremony, the minister borrowed rings from the bride and groom's parents, which was a creative and touching move. Andre and Stephanie joyously married, they were certainly not doomed. Rather, they were almost immediately blessed with their own bundle of joy, who they named Ringo.

Not every couple wants ten children to be in their wedding party, but if you are considering having a very young child be your ring bearer or flower girl, be sure you lower your expectations! Be ready to skip the child's walk down the aisle if he or she is not in the mood for it. And remember, the younger the child, the less predictable their performance. Some tips:

1. Never put your actual rings on the ring bearer's pillow. It will come with two plastic rings tied to it. Leave those on for show, and let the best man and best woman carry the wedding bands.
2. Allow young children to walk down the aisle but don't expect them to stand at the altar. Have someone they know and will go to. Let that person catch them when they get to the front. Ask them to either sit with the kids or take them out of the room.
3. Do not have a child and his/her parent in the same wedding party! Either the parent will be distracted by the child's behavior or the child will see the parent and cry for him/her.
4. Never assign care-taking of children to a close relative! They want to watch you get married, not have to pull a screaming child out of the room.
5. Best of all, as much as you love your nieces and nephews, don't exploit their cuteness. It could ruin your wedding day!

CHAPTER 33
PHOTO DILEMMA

Maybe the photographer or videographer is doing a terrible job: missing important moments, texting during the ceremony, or fumbling with his equipment. Maybe they aren't doing what you asked them to do. For example, you wanted lots of candid shots but your cameraman is all about the posed set-ups. It could also be that they are not doing their job at all. For instance, you've hired them to capture the most memorable moments of your day, and they are taking pictures of Uncle Frank's new girlfriend. Or instead of shooting your dear' dad getting down on the dance floor, they are having a drink at the bar. Maybe they get lazy half way through the day and take the most convenient pictures from their position at the dinner table. Do your research to find a professional who knows what they are doing.

A few years ago, I attended a wedding of a close family friend. It was a very small intimate wedding of about fifty people. There was an amateur photographer - a family friend with a really nice camera. Apart from myself, I noticed that no one else was taking pictures. Very strange, I thought, and I continued to snap away. I took pictures of the ceremony, the bridal party, but most pictures were of myself standing in the garden. At the end of the night, I had taken about twenty pictures of what was truly a lovely wedding.

About three days later, I got a frantic call from the bride's mother. Apparently, the photographer had accidentally deleted all of the pictures. The entire family, especially the bride, was in a state of panic.

"How did she manage to do that?" I asked.

The stressed-out mother of the bride explained what happened and told me that she was in desperate need of my pictures. They were the only memory of that day. I did not hesitate to develop them immediately and give them to her. Everyone was so relieved.

A colleague of mine shared this story with me. He wasn't hired to do the filming, and he couldn't believe the couple wanted to scrimp on the photography during what was a pretty extravagant wedding. As a professional, he knew what to look for, and he was appalled by George, a relative the couple enlisted to take pictures.

George loved to talk. Whether it is to one person or a huge crowd, George just liked to be the center of attention. George was also a budding photographer who enjoyed taking pictures of his friends and his beloved animals. He was very excited when his cousin asked him to take the pictures for her wedding.

George concentrated hard at the ceremony and got fairly good shots of the couple at all the right moments. The things he missed, he staged afterward, just like a professional would. He looked like he was working hard, but he acted as if he knew what he was doing.

Things went downhill once he arrived at the reception. As soon as George got there, he spotted friends and family members. As they greeted one another, they sparked up a conversation that lasted for about an hour. George was totally caught up in conversation and missed some great shots.

As the wedding progressed, George continued talking to other guests and took a picture or two in between conversations. He laughed and joked and even danced with some of the guests. He had a great night, and to any observer, he looked like a guest - part of the fun. It was a difficult role – to be both a family member (and invited guest) who was doubling as the photographer.

By the end of the night, George was looking nervous. How many pictures could this guy have taken? Definitely not as many as he could have, not as many as a professional would have shot. George tried to gather family groups together for pictures, but by that time, everyone was away from their tables, milling around and dancing. His timing was off.

He followed the bride and groom around for the last hour of the night, but there was no way he made up for the hours he had missed.

We haven't seen the album, nor heard complaints from the bride, but if she had George to cut costs – as we suspect she did – she couldn't have much to complain about.

If you are budget conscious, consider other ways to get all of the photos you want. You can ask several friends who love to post pictures on Facebook to be your informal photographers – more hands make light work!

Challenge everyone to use their phones to take the cutest selfies of the people around them and with the bride and groom. Post the "winner" on your Facebook page.

Make it a game and ask them to forward you any videos or pictures that came out particularly well, unusual, or funny. With technology on your side, even without a professional photographer or videographer, you should be able to get some valuable shots worthy of your photo album

CHAPTER 34
CUSTOMS, RITES, AND WRONGS

Some of the most beautiful weddings are those which show how two cultures come together in the union of the bride and groom. It might be a sensitive issue as to what specific customs you include. With care and respect, and perhaps with guidance from relatives, officiants and other experts in wedding customs, both cultures can be represented with honor and dignity. Perhaps the first half of the ceremony can represent one culture and the second half the other.

Or, maybe one culture can be represented in the ceremony and the other in the reception. Or you might combine the two elements throughout. It is an exciting and beautiful thing to share different cultural traditions with your guests, but be sure they have a guide of some kind if they are completely foreign to it.

If you want to incorporate cultural elements into your wedding but you are not from that particular culture, make sure that you do your research. The last thing you want to do is to disrespect your partner's traditions or present something that you don't fully understand. For example, if you are not from India, but want to have an Indian themed wedding because that is where you first met and fell in love, make sure that you are making an accurate representation. Go to the library, ask questions, or go online to get specific information. It is a good idea to explain the traditions and symbols of your ceremony so that all your guests understand what is going on.

I shot the wedding of Nidya and Hakeem and asked a lot of questions myself so that I could be in the right place at the right time, filming the most meaningful of the various elements of the day.

Nidya and Hakeem were planning a beautiful multicultural wedding. Nidya was from India, and Hakeem was from Nigeria. They were both very excited to be bringing their families together for a cultural extravaganza. Although the planning was enjoyable, at times, it was a bit stressful. Nidya and Hakeem often disagreed on elements of the wedding. They disagreed on the music, the food, the décor, the dress. Nidya wanted Indian music, but Hakeem wanted Nigerian. Nidya wanted the main dish to be curry, but Hakeem wanted fufu. Neither had even tried each other's favorite dish, but they insisted they didn't want to have it at the wedding.

In order to squash the battle and move the wedding planning along, Nidya's mother came up with the brilliant idea.

"Why don't you prepare the traditional dishes for each other?" she said, "Nidya, let Hakeem try the curry. I'll help you make a lovely curry for him!"

"Mother, it's a great idea, but I don't think he'll even taste it!" Nidya said.

"Then you will have trials in your marriage if he won't even try a sample of a dish for your wedding!" her mother said. "Propose he try it and tell him you will do the same with his dish."

"All right.

But, I confess, I don't even know what fufu is." Nidya said.

"Well, that is the first thing to find out then, my dear!"

Nidya did her research but was not comforted.

"Ay, Mother, fufu is eaten with your fingers!" she said.

"And for Hakeem's family and friends that will be perfectly natural." Her mother said.

One night, Nidya surprised Hakeem with a heavenly curry that her mother helped her to prepare.

"This is what I would like to serve at the wedding," she said.

Hakeem had tasted curry before – and had this argument before, too.

"It's wonderful, Nidya, darling, but…"

"Stop! I know what you are going to say. I'll try your dish, too. Would you make it for me for dinner tomorrow?"

"Of course! You've never even tried it before!" he said.

I know. And, whether I enjoy it or not, I wanted to ask you if maybe we could have both dishes – the curry and the fufu at the wedding. But maybe we could round it out with some American traditions too. You know, a fish choice or something." Nidya said.

Hakeem agreed to think about it and ate the curry hungrily. The following night, as agreed, he prepared fufu for his bride, and she was pleasantly surprised by how much she enjoyed it. With her fear put aside, she felt more certain than ever that both foods could be served at the wedding. They even went so far as to leave off the American dish and serve the two favorites "family style" at each guest table. They reasoned that this would expose their very different cultures to each other's families.

The difficulty was going to be their American friends and wedding party members. Both Hakeem and Nidya had chosen friends to be in their wedding parties who were completely unfamiliar with either culture.

On the night of the pre-wedding, Hakeem and Nidya decided Indian traditions would prevail. That culture had called for a party where the two families met and celebrated with food and dancing. At the close of the evening, a Pundit would ask a prayer of blessing for a long and happy marriage for the couple.

Sarah and Andrew, a bridesmaid and her husband, both Protestants from the Midwest were like fish out of water on the eve of the wedding. They felt like the only two not wearing colorful ceremonial dress. They resisted the ethnic food choices and didn't dance because they felt self-conscious, not knowing the protocol or liking the music. Nidya noticed their discomfort and tried to explain the customs, but after a while, she gave up as her relatives called her for the many small traditions of the night. The bride couldn't be preoccupied on her wedding eve!

On the wedding day, which was to be a blend of Nigerian and Indian customs, Hakeem opted not to wear the turban and veil traditional for an Indian groom, and instead, wore a garment typical for his country, along with a handsome headpiece. Nidya was lovely in a brilliantly colored gown, her hands painted with henna tattoos signifying blessings of wealth, happiness, and luck.

For each side of the family there were programs explaining the traditions but it wasn't enough to ease the discomfort of Sarah or Andrew. They stood when they were told to stand, and they picked at their food during the three-day festivities. They felt it was all a little "too much" – a wedding that took three days to complete.

The couple opted for wedding bands in the tradition of their adopted home in America instead of the tying of the Margala Sutra which is derived from India, or the tying of a cloth knot, which was African and the origin of the saying "tying the knot" in western countries. Instead, gold bands would be symbols of their bond and their vows.

The dinner tables were beautifully laid out with the favorite traditional dishes of both Nigeria and India, and the food sparked conversation. Everyone shared stories of customs from their own cultures. Unfortunately, Sarah and Andrew were not fans of curry and refused to use their hands to eat the fufu. It did not endear them to the family members from either side.

To cap the three-day-long festivities, on the day after the wedding, Hakeem went to his in-law's house and took away his bride to live happily ever after. On the following Monday, everyone returned to work at their offices in Manhattan. Sarah and Andrew, relieved to see their friends in western dress and wearing conventional wedding rings, were finally able to laugh at their geeky discomfort and ask about the traditions that had confused and alienated them.

"What was up with you running around and racing to your seats at the wedding?" Andrew asked.

Nidya grinned. "Ah, that race was to see who would rule the household!" Smiling at Hakeem, she continued, "How great that I won!"

Whether it is simply wearing a bit of thistle on your gown to symbolize your Scottish roots, or going full out with a three-day multicultural blowout, don't be too attached to outcomes, and be very flexible with people who won't understand or appreciate your efforts. When Danielle tied her family's tartan over the shoulder of her wedding gown, people wondered why she would ruin the look of the lovely dress. Really, as long as they aren't being required to wear it, why does it matter?

Let your vendors, officiants, and other personnel know what to expect and what you want to highlight during your wedding so nobody will be confused and try to correct something that isn't wrong!

CHAPTER 35
LIGHTS GO OUT BEFORE VOWS

Everyone has certain superstitions, and many of us look for signs and symbols in the world around us. Sometimes, nervousness causes us to see messages that are only in our imagination...

It was a hot summer afternoon in New Jersey – the kind of day any bride would be thrilled to celebrate on her wedding day. Craig, the groom, was African-American and Toya, the bride, was Haitian-American. Both sets of families came from cultural backgrounds full of superstitious beliefs. Both worked in Manhattan -- Craig as a banker with CITI group, and Toya as a project manager in her company. They had been together for 6 years.

On the big day, family, friends, and colleagues gathered at the church. The wedding party looked sharp: the groomsmen were all tall – taller than I'd ever seen. I believe the shortest man among them was 6'2. They were bankers, businessmen, and professional athletes. They all looked good, and I could tell by their wristwatches, cufflinks, and shoes that they all did well financially, easily making six-figure salaries.

The bridesmaids and groomsmen were a glamorous parade of beauty and elegance. The sight of them had all of the single men and ladies giggling in admiration. It was like watching a movie that you didn't want to end.

Everything went according to plan. The maid of honor and the best man walked in. Then the flower girl and the ring bearer, who, unlike the rest of the party, was Caucasian. He was a cute little seven-year-old boy.

The priest preached an excellent sermon, and when the time for the vows came, and everyone was waiting for the "I do" moment, the priest said to the groom:

"Do you take this woman to be your wife, for better or worse, until death do you part?"

Before he could answer, the church was plunged into pitch darkness. The power had gone out throughout the entire neighborhood. The only light coming into the building was in little traces from the skylights in the ceiling and through the narrow windows. The people in the room drew in a collective gasp. Was it a sign?

My journalistic instinct told me to shoot the story the way it was unfolding, which was not necessarily the way the newlyweds would have wanted. Possibly, it wouldn't be retained in their final editing, but I turned on my camera light to focus on the faces of the couple who had been about to take their vows.

The expressions on the faces of the bride and groom were similar – they were both in a state of shock. Around them, members of the wedding party, family members, and church staff were running up and down the aisles, frantic to do something.

I turned my focus to the bride who looked disappointed and confused. It was as though I heard her saying," Oh my God what is this? Could this be a sign? What will people say about this omen?"

The bride looked at the groom, who smiled encouragingly. People crowded around to comfort her while she stood, in shock, trying to figure why the lights went out right at the point when he should have been saying, "I do." Why at this moment and not before the walk down the aisle? Why right before he was to take his vow? The groom came close to console her, telling her that everything would be all right, but she was on a different frequency.

Sweat dripped down her face, and her friends blotted her with a tissue so as not to mess up her makeup. The whole situation went on for what seemed like a lifetime, but I realized when the lights suddenly came back on that they had only been out for two minutes. Normalcy restored, I looked at the bride who seemed to me to be pretending to be happy, realizing all eyes were on her – as they should be on her wedding day. She took on the persona of a happy, blushing bride, but I could see that she was still shaking.

Making a lame joke, the priest resumed his place and continued the service. It seemed that he understood the bride's fears and superstitions, talking about how this would be a moment no one would forget and downplaying the whispers about bad luck or a sign from God.

Though she and her beloved completed their vows, exchanged their rings, and recessed up the aisle to beautiful music and the sound of applause, I could see the bride was not herself. Her smiles were for the camera, for appearances, but there were the traces of tears on her face and a quiver to her lips.

I found it touching to see the groom look at her so tenderly and squeeze her close when they reached the door, just out of sight of the congregation. I could not hear what he whispered to her, but she looked up at him with a hopeful expression. I like to think she was listening and trying hard to believe the words of reassurance he gave her. I will never know as I was too far away to adjust his microphone so that the exchange might be picked up. It was a private moment, and one I hope made the difference to her.

The couple received their guests at the church door, and over the twenty minutes it took to get everyone outside and ready to throw birdseed, I saw the tension leave the bride's face slowly with each person's warm congratulations. It was my prayer that no one reinforced her superstitious fears.

It was not until well into the reception when the couple was introduced for the first time as "Mr. and Mrs." that I saw the bride relax, as if she finally accepted the fact that they were officially married. Bad luck or not, the success of their union rested firmly in their hands from that point on. I wished the best for them.

There are plenty of things that can wreck your wedding day, but don't let signs, omens, or superstitions be one of them. If you have a superstitious bone in your body, there are a few things you can do. If you are having an outdoor wedding, don't light a Unity candle unless you have a hurricane shade to put over it to prevent it from blowing out. Better yet, do a sand ceremony instead. If you worry you might trip, don't wear high heels. If you worry that it will rain, and you see that as bad luck, remember that in Hawaii, it is good luck to have rain on your wedding day!

Turn the story you tell yourself into something positive, so that no matter what happens, you will have a day of celebration. Luck comes through your intention. Make it so!

CHAPTER 36
MOCKING BIRDS

What considerations go into making the guest list? Seeing what I've seen, it's a mystery to me why certain individuals are invited to weddings, or even considered friends when their behavior is anything but friendly, or kind, or even humane.

One wedding, in particular, had the cattiest group of women I have ever seen in all my years of filming weddings.

They arrived together, in a gaggle. They wore, not exactly the same dress, but a variation of the same dress: black, short, tight. In some cases, TOO tight, if you know what I mean.

They arrived early and found what they must have thought was the best possible seats, making themselves visible to all, from all angles, and while being seen, they were able to see everything. They sat and began a running commentary. Nothing escaped their notice. The size of the church, the pew bows, the flowers.

"Could she spend ten dollars on the arrangements?"

"Go see if those are carnations or peonies. I bet they're carnations!"

They snorted laughter.

As each guest arrived, the women sized them up. They paid special attention to the males. They declared their verdict: handsome man, ugly man. Well dressed. The poorly matched with his escort. Whether with a woman or not, every guy was discussed as a fruit ripe for the plucking. I noted that not one of the women had come with a date of her own.

I took shots of the gathering crowd, of the altar and the flowers whose value the ladies had questioned. Then finished, I stationed myself near them, because after all, they truly did have a great view of the whole space and they were very amusing to listen to.

When the honored guests were seated by the stately junior groomsmen, grandmother, god-mother, and then the mothers of the groom and bride, the women tried to stifle their cackles but were not altogether successful. And they kept talking.

"Oh my Gawd! Could you find more shades of puke green?"

"Honey, that's one mustard yellow, not green!

Baby-diarrhea yellow!"

They saved their best remarks for the bridesmaids.

"I am seeing way more of her than I want to see!"

"That is one big butt on her – and all wrapped in satin!" They all cracked up and continued to roll out commentaries on each girl as she walked slowly down the aisle. It would have been quite humiliating had they heard them. I hoped they didn't.

The moment for the bride's entrance came and everyone stood. Now the girls couldn't see quite as well, so the next comments were delayed.

"She did not!" one of them said with snorts of laughter.

"Sleeves. Who is she, Princess Kate now?" They snickered with their shoulders shaking.

"Long sleeves on arms like that?

The pillars on my front porch are smaller!"

"And a neckline? What neckline?"

"It's a turtleneck-line!" They burst out laughing.

Around them, people were starting to turn and frown at them. I even heard one or two "shushes."

Just as the bride walked past, there was an awkward moment when the organist paused. Maybe the sheet music had blown away, or the man lost his place. In that short silence, everyone, most especially the bride, could hear,

"My Gawd! What does he see in her?!"

The bride's head swiveled in the direction of the voice. Her smile wavered. On her arm, her father encouraged her to keep walking, to ignore it. The organist resumed playing, and with only a tiny misstep, the bride continued up the aisle.

For a moment I panned my camera to the women, who I misjudged. I really believed they would be sorry and shut up. But, I was wrong. I caught them just at the moment when they broke into peals of laughter, almost as loud as the surging organ itself. I stealthily moved to film the ceremony, hoping that the bride could put this indignity behind her.

It is worth it to go over your guest list and reject anyone you thought of inviting because your family wanted you to, or because you're related. Don't just have people because you feel obligated or nostalgic.

Weddings are a weird crossroad. The changes that come with married life mean the couple outgrows certain people. It can be because priorities shift, or you're just at a different life-phase than somebody else. For example, having kids change up your life, your schedule and your energy. You associate less with people who are busy doing other things: like hanging out or focusing on a career.

Sometimes, the reason you leave friends behind after a wedding is because of how they behaved or (shallow) the size of the gift they gave you! Thinking about the cackling ghouls in the preceding story, I don't see *any reason* at all to keep them in your circle, relatives or not!

When you are making your guest list, be sure the people you spend $65. 00 a plate on will be in your life long-term. If you doubt your relationship status, leave them off the list and send them a postcard from your honeymoon instead!

CHAPTER 37
ENOUGH FOOD (POISONING) FOR ALL

There is nothing quite as disappointing as bland, typical catering-hall food at a wedding reception. Sadly, most of us have come to expect it. But, when the food is terrible and guests even fear for their health when eating it, then you really have a problem.

You would never expect it from the looks of the venue. The place was gorgeous, but the kitchen staff and protocol left something to be desired. Desiree and Joseph chose the best of the appetizers and passable fish, chicken, and beef choices. The food wasn't stellar, but they were on a budget, and they felt the meal would be comparable to a nice, if not four-star Michelin-rated, restaurant.

On the wedding day, the very last thing on Desiree and Joseph's minds was food. The couple missed their cocktail hour, which happens so often when there are photos to be shot and a dress to change out of. Small plates and drinks were brought up to the bridal suite, but everyone was too busy and excited to do much more than guzzle champagne and nibble the cheese and crackers. If a few bites of the cheese were hard, well, everyone reasoned it had sat out during an hour of picture-taking. No harm done. The flies on the salami went unnoticed. No one commented that there was no ice under the crudité.

In the fullness of time, the bridal party was announced by the DJ, and they danced into the hall as they had rehearsed. It was a great scene to shoot.

The guests went wild, and the music pumped up louder while lights flashed and everyone got up to dance. After the excitement of the grand entrance, the DJ asked everyone to find their seats and get ready for the toasts. In the lull, as waiters began to take orders, conversation about the cocktail hour could be heard,

"I wouldn't touch that shrimp."

"I know, it had a terrible ammonia odor!"

From another table:

"I had to spit out the chicken satay; I swear it was raw in the middle."

"I don't think the fruit had been refrigerated for hours.

It was just limp!"

"I tried that fruit. You're right, it was warm. It even had a tang to it – I think it was going off."

The menu cards on the table were elegant, and the guests would be right to get their hopes up for a delicious meal. Around the table, they gave their orders to the quiet and attentive wait staff.

In no time, the salads were set in front of everyone. What should have been "fresh wild greens" were actually blackened, soft petals of tired lettuce soaked in a watery dressing. I couldn't help but take a few shots of them. People pushed their plates aside and reached for the bread baskets.

"This bread has mold on it!"

That statement echoed from several tables. Though the waiters were asked for more bread, there was no more to be brought. The bride and groom flitted from table to table, greeting guests. They were blissfully unaware of the food disaster that was unfolding all around them.

Finally, the dinner plates came out of the kitchen. Each dish was elegantly covered with a silver dome that the waiters took off with a flourish before each guest. Overall, the presentation of the meal was lovely, and people tucked into their food with gusto.

"Oh! Be careful! The fish had bones!"

From another table across the room:

"They didn't debone this fish, jeez, I almost choked!"

And at the head table,

"Why is the edge of this chicken gray like that?"

"Wow, I didn't see that. Take off the gravy and look: mine has that weird gray on it too."

"Was it microwaved?"

"I don't know, it doesn't seem burned, maybe it's undercooked?"

"Well, don't eat the clam sauce!"

"What clam sauce? I didn't see that as one of the choices."

"Thank God, you're right. Bad clams will kill ya!" Everyone laughed at that as they pushed their plates away. The longer the plates sat, the more the potatoes congealed into the green beans, which came preserved in some sort of aspic.

Even people who had ordered the beef only picked at their food, nervous that there was more than a bad taste to follow them home.

The bride noticed her mother's full plate.

"What's wrong? Why aren't you eating?" she asked.

"Honestly, Desiree, did you try the food here before you put down your deposit?" her mother said.

"Of course we did –" Desiree's face reddened. "Honey," she said to the groom, "maybe you should speak with the maître d'?"

Of course there was nothing to be done at this point. Guests had hunted down the last of the breadsticks and had filled up on bar fruit and additional glasses of wine. The party got louder and louder as a result, and some people joked about ordering pizza.

The groom managed to arrange a discount, pointing out the moldy bread and brandishing the spoiled shrimp.

"You could have killed off half of my new in-laws,"

The groom groused.

"And in two years' time, you might've thanked me,"

The manager replied.

The couple and the management agreed that they would serve the cake early since people were hungry. The cake came from a well-respected baker in town, so it was safe from the catering hall's culinary ineptitude. They offered to put vanilla ice cream on it for the couple as a way to make amends. Wisely, the bride and groom declined.

You want your guests to be well-fed, but if you are on a budget, sometimes corners have to be cut. If the food is adequate, no harm done, but unhealthy practices are dangerous. See if you can get a kitchen tour and check for cleanliness. Call the health department and see if there have been violations or warnings. And, most of all, go online and look for reviews, referrals, and comments from other bridal couples. It could save a lot of anxiety (and food poisoning!).

CHAPTER 38
STAINED AND STRAINED

Flexibility will always stand you in good stead, especially on your wedding day. The bride with the need to control every aspect of the day, the woman who has the image of what will be "perfect" runs the risk of the greatest disappointment. This scenario is a "perfect" example.

Colleen was a natural red-head; tall, fit, and beautiful in a pale sort of way. As an attorney, she had very low tolerance for sub-par performance in her professional life, and she expected only the best in her personal life as well. Colleen's wedding would be no exception.

Derek, the groom, was an inch shorter than Colleen and quieter. Handsome and intelligent, if he had opinions about his wedding day, he did not mention them. During meetings with the bride and groom, it was clear that it was Colleen's show and imperfection would not be tolerated. The highest performance standards were expected, and the day must go off without a hitch. All of the professionals surrounding this wedding were on alert: they'd better be at their best.

The rehearsal went very well as the bride controlled every move made by her attendants, the groomsmen, and the groom himself. She stopped just short of directing the paid contractors, but she made many requests and suggestions for lighting, floral and other decorations, music, and the placement of her bridal party.

She implied that if she wasn't satisfied, contracts, compensation, and gratuities were all going to be reconsidered. We understood: we had promises to keep if we intended to get paid. As long as everyone complied, the bride's pale smile did not waver. I could tell behind all the bossiness, she was nervous. Her smile never quite reached her eyes.

We had all been advised that lateness would not be tolerated. Colleen had made it clear that not a moment of the reception would be wasted by delays of any sort. So, alarm bells began to sound when the bride's limousine was fifteen minutes late on the wedding day. When the car pulled up, we all rushed outside to greet the bride and usher her into the venue. Myself, the photographer, coordinator, maître d', the officiant, and several members of the wedding party clustered around the car door. A palpable case of the jitters affected all of us. Colleen must be kept calm and happy, and this late start was putting us all at a disadvantage.

As the bride swung her legs out of the car, everyone saw it at the same time: a bright red blotch on the otherwise perfect gleaming ivory gown. Collectively our eyes moved upward from the stain on the dress to the face of the bride. Rather than composed and pale, Colleen's visage was grim and flushed.

"My nephew spilled ketchup on my dress." Her teeth were clenched, and her lips barely moved.

The three-year-old culprit – the ring bearer – was squirming madly behind the bride, impatient to get out of the car. His mother, the matron of honor, was doing her best to hold him back.

Colleen stepped regally out of the limousine, and we all fell in around her: holding up her gown, opening the door, taking her elbow; each of us doing our best, instinctively, to stave off the explosion.

The maître d' had experience of flustered brides. He called one of his servers over and gave her instructions. Seltzer water was on its way. We got Colleen situated in the bridal suite, attended to her dress and removed the stain for the most part, while helping her to focus on what was most important: marrying her beloved Derek, with or without the glitches.

Sadly, it's the brides who most need things to go perfectly who wind up having the roughest wedding days. To control for any more mishaps, we took the actual wedding ring off the ring bearer's pillow and gave it to the best man to hold. Finally, the wedding party got into their places, and the bride, at the end of the procession, took her father's arm.

"OK, Dad, don't forget to shake Derek's hand and give me a kiss before you go sit down."

"Yes, Colleen, dear, I remember," Colleen's father replied.

The wedding party was large and handsome, and everyone played their part to perfection. The ring bearer made it down the aisle and was scooped up by his grandfather to sit in the front row. The flower girls tossed rose petals. The junior bridesmaid stayed back to receive the elbow-length gloves that the bride would remove before taking the groom's hand.

Our collective nervousness had died down by the time the party had made their entrances. They made it look easy, and it only remained for Colleen to make it safely down the aisle. It was not to be. Taking ten steps into the hall, we could see that something was wrong.

The back of Colleen's head was not moving along with her body. She seemed to be arching back. I honestly didn't know whether to film it or not. It was not a dramatic moment, but an embarrassing one. Then we could hear her hissing,

"Dad. You are stepping on my train."

The cathedral-length lace train was affixed to Colleen's head in an elaborate hairdo quite different from the more popular and casual styles I usually see these days. It was braided, combed, and fairly well embedded into her hair. She could not move another step until her father realized he was walking on her train. A bridesmaid ran to the rescue. She moved the father of the bride off the train then fluffed it. She came around to the front of Colleen and yanked the entire headpiece back down an inch or so lower over Colleen's forehead before dashing back to her place on the altar.

Colleen replaced her steely smile and resumed her walk down the aisle. She stopped about ten feet from the groom. Her matron of honor took the bouquet, and Colleen peeled the elegant glove from her right arm and handed it dramatically to the junior bridesmaid. Unfortunately, she forgot to remove the large bracelet on her left wrist, so that glove came halfway off and would go no further.

The officiant stepped forward, sweating.

"Colleen, it's OK, let's just leave the glove on for now."

It was a ridiculous thing to say, but he just wanted to get through the ceremony. Colleen's expression did not change as she rolled the glove back up her arm.

The ceremony was touching because of the sweet sensitivity of the groom, whose encouragement and heartfelt vows made the bride smile in earnest. By the time the ring exchange began, Colleen seemed almost relaxed. The minister said,

"Please take Derek's ring, place it on his left hand and say…"

Colleen took the ring from the best man and as she tried to put it on the groom, it slipped out of her gloved fingers and bounced under the first row of pews. Her eyes widened. As her face crumbled, Colleen seemed younger and softer. She let her tears fall and her expectations go. It would be a memorable wedding day, but not because it was perfect!

The ring was found and put on the groom's finger. He couldn't put Colleen's ring on because of the glove she couldn't take off. At this point, all Colleen could do was laugh. We all laughed with her.

At the recessional, the woman who walked up the aisle arm in arm with her groom was more tear-stained and less starched than the woman who had rehearsed here the night before. Yet, we knew she was also happier, and maybe, wiser.

Approach your wedding day with flexibility and let go of your expectations. Laughter is a better lubricant than tears!

CHAPTER 39
INSECURE BRIDE

Some brides will do anything to have the perfect wedding. They will spare no expense and put themselves through all sorts of treatments. They will squeeze themselves into body-torturing garments to achieve the bridal look they are after. And sometimes, it still isn't enough. They will compare themselves to others and take other's cold remarks to heart. How tragic when they are criticized by the people who they thought were their friends.

"I didn't eat for a year," Tracy said proudly to the stylist doing her maid of honor's hair. I'd been laughing at the unbelievable stories they'd been swapping about how crazy brides could get leading up to their wedding day.

"How much did you lose?" asked the stylist?

"Twenty."

"That's not so much."

"I also went to the gym every day. I worked with a trainer three times a week!"

The stylist nodded, not impressed. She looked Tracy over, from head to foot.

"My trainer was written up in the New York Post last week. He cost me $300. 00 a session!" Tracy said.

"I'm glad I didn't have to do any of that for my wedding day," said the stylist.

"Well, you look great, Tracy," the maid of honor, Deidre said, trying to keep the peace. She watched her sister's reaction.

The bride frowned. Everyone in the room knew she had dieted down to a perfect size four in order to fit into the ivory, sweetheart-neckline, princess-style gown she had selected. She had chosen the Baracci dress after seeing Beyoncé in it in a video. It wasn't like any of the dresses her bridal attendants tried to talk her into. Plus, it was more money and more glitzy than anything they had worn on their wedding days. She had spared no effort or expense to have a more over-the-top wedding day than any of her friends. She made a point to mention all of these things – several times. Even I was sick of hearing about it.

We were in the Presidential Suite in the city's finest hotel, getting ready for the wedding, which would be held shortly in the banquet hall downstairs. The door opened, and a waiter entered with a bar cart, followed by a server with a tray of food. They laid out plates of hot and cold appetizers and bottles of wine, champagne, beer and soda.

"Wow! This is as nice as some cocktail hours I've been to!" one of the bridesmaids said.

From across the room another woman commented,

"So you couldn't get all the way down to the weight you wanted. It's OK, Trace."

"Shhh, Hilary, stop!" said Deidre, but it was too late. Tracy's eyes flashed.

"What's that supposed to mean? This is what a woman's body looks like Hilary!"

Hilary, who happened to be very thin, rolled her eyes. She picked up some hot antipasti.

"Curvy is in anyway, Tracy," she said.

The stylist snickered. She finished up on the maid of honor and turned back to the bride who was standing looking at herself sidewise in the mirror. She sucked in her stomach, pulled back her shoulders.

"Let me fix your makeup," the stylist said.

That took Tracy's attention off her waistline. She whirled around to face the stylist, panic in her eyes.

"Why? What's the matter? My makeup is done!"

"Oh, OK…" the stylist said.

"What? Wait! It's my eyes!" Tracy squinted at her reflection then her voice became childish and demanding.

"It's not right! Fix it, fix it!" She started to cry, looking more like an insecure little girl than a 28-year-old bride.

Down the row of chairs, Hilary snorted.

"There she goes," she said.

"I wanted my eyes to look like Kim K's," Tracy said. "Not all smoky-eye but big lashes, you know?"

"Tracy, your eyes are fine. Go get dressed so we can see how you look," Deidre said.

When Tracy swept back into the room a few minutes later, looking like a bombshell, the other girls' ohh'd and ahh'd over her gown.

"I still can't believe you went with that one," Hilary said.

The stylist stood next to Hilary, and they both looked Tracy up and down. "I see what you mean," she said, and Hilary nodded.

"You see what she has *us* wearing?" Hilary said. She indicated the navy-blue gowns the wedding party wore.

The dresses were elegant but simple.

"Well, Hilary, I didn't want it to be like your wedding. Those bridesmaids' dresses were so beautiful that your wedding gown didn't stand out at all," Tracy smiled sweetly.

The stylist snorted and now turned and watched for Hilary's reaction.

"Just one of those dresses cost more than all these put together," Hilary said.

"I knew I wasted a ton of money on that dress," Tracy said.

"My dress was beautiful and not a hot mess like that thing you're wearing!" Hilary stood up, taking a wide stance and putting her hands on her hips. She leaned toward Tracy menacingly. Tracy squared off and faced Hilary, not backing down.

The stylist stepped back and out of the way.

"Look, this is my day. You might be my future sister-in-law, but I don't have to take your crap at my wedding. My wedding cost more than yours and your sister's combined! I have more class and – "Tracy said.

Deirdre cut her off, "Tracy, listen. We're about to go to the church. Let's all just calm down."

Fortunately, there were two limos picking up members of the wedding party and family from the hotel. Tracy insisted that Hilary ride with her mother-in-law and meet them at the church. In the end, Hilary attended the ceremony and left shortly thereafter. She did not stand up in the wedding party as planned.

Her brother, the groom, never entirely understood what had happened, but when he saw the bill for his bride's over-the-top, better-than-anybody-else's wedding, I hear that he nearly had a heart attack.

Focus on what you want, and don't let anyone make you feel like less than you are. I always say that tension shows up in your video and photos, so surround yourself with positivity, and keep smiling. It's your day, and nobody can "wreck" it but you!

CHAPTER 40
MOTHER – OUT - LAWS

I am hired to film brides and grooms, but frequently the family members command my attention. Often, it is not for sweet, unforgettably touching moments, but for bad behavior!

Mandy called her future mother-in-law "the Dragon Lady" and her father-in-law "Mr. Nobody."

I overheard her several times just in the short span I was with her. I could see why she did. Imelda wore a mandarin-collared dress and she seemed -- even to me -- to be difficult, opinionated and critical. Father-in-law, Bob, was stooped and quiet as if he wanted to be invisible.

Mandy was polite, trying to be the nice girl Imelda wanted for her son. But just watching, I could tell she was never going to win. At the rehearsal, she wore something prim, and Imelda commented on it. Until she took off her sweater; then her sleeveless dress got a raised eyebrow and an evening full of snide remarks. I watched as her fiancé Jeffrey became exasperated, not with his mother, but with Mandy for making a bad impression.

Jeffrey clearly bowed to his mother. To be fair though, Mandy seemed to do the same with both her parents. In comparison to Imelda and Bob, Mandy's mother and father were cuddly dolls. Where Imelda was tall and slim with a regal bearing and a British accent, Mavis was pillowy, short and round.

Where Bob was quiet and unassuming, Roger had a booming voice and a gregarious personality. Where Imelda was impersonal, Mavis was everybody's second mom.

Where Bob went unnoticed, Roger made friends instantly and seemed to be constantly introducing new friends to one another – sincerely wanting everyone to connect and find common ground.

"My parents love you," I heard Jeffrey say to Mandy at more than one point during the rehearsal and the following dinner.

"Ha! Prove it!" she said.

Mandy didn't have to reassure her fiancé that her parents loved him. They lavished Jeffrey with attention all night. I'm sure they'd been calling him "Son" before they were engaged.

The parents of the couple had never met before the night of the rehearsal – and it was a disaster. Sitting stiffly in the back of the church, Imelda and Bob watched the proceedings.

They were old-school Catholics and sure that the roof would fall in because they were in a Protestant church. They'd secretly gone to their priest for his blessing and assurance that they wouldn't go to hell by entering a different church.

The minister, unfortunately for him, did not rehearse the entrance of the mothers of the bride or groom. To him, it was straight forward: groom's mother walks in, the bride's mother walks in, then the processional begins. To him, getting the mothers, fathers, and grandparents seated was a formality.

At the end of the rehearsal, as everyone casually stood around chatting, Imelda raised her voice. Directing herself to the minister, who was standing with the bride, she said loudly,

"Excuse me! When are we expected to enter?"

"And you are?" the minister said.

The bride gasped, knowing her mother-in-law would see it as disrespectful. "That's Jeff's parents. The GROOM'S MOTHER!" she said. She immediately turned to Imelda and started to apologize and explain and dissemble and basically grovel.

"And, am I to sit in the front to watch my son get married, or shall I sit back here and keep quiet?"

"Mom, No! Of course not!" Jeffrey said.

Mandy looked at her mother and saw her roll her eyes. If you told Mavis she had to sit in the back she would probably grab three cousins and giggle the whole time. She'd make it the best seat in the house.

Imelda lit into the minister, scolding him for his disrespect. She stood tall and actually advanced on the poor man. He was a big guy but shriveled under her attack. The entire wedding party gaped in horror. No one knew what to do or say. A couple of the bridesmaids took pictures, and I imagined them posting on Facebook with comments like, "Dragon Lady on fire!"

"Bob, come. We're leaving." Imelda said, beckoning to her husband. He shrugged and followed her out the door. Jeffrey ran after them, calling them to wait.

"Oh brother!" Mandy said. Her parents came to her side.

"Don't worry sweetheart. There is always a little drama! It is better tonight than on the wedding day. Let her get it out of her system. She is losing a lovely son to my daughter!" Mavis said.

"Mandy, Mandy, let me go see what I can do!" her father Roger said in a sing-song voice.

He started off, full of confidence that he could fix everything.

"Dad! No. Let Jeff talk to her." Mandy said. Then, turning to her mother, she said,

"What a crazy thing to say, Mama! You don't think you're losing me to him, do you?"

"Oh, no, I'm gaining a son! It's all in how you look at it. Now! Let's get to the restaurant!" Mavis said.

Jeffrey dragged his parents to the dinner. They sat next to Mandy's parents, but no one could engage Imelda in conversation. Bob focused on his plate.

I saw the awkwardness. Mandy was watching her mother, who was watching Imelda. I couldn't imagine Mavis thinking anything but how to defuse the tension. She seemed to be a lover and not a fighter.

I watched Mandy's father going from person to person, getting everyone talking, putting everyone at ease. Bob kept eating quietly. What a family, I thought.

The wedding was scheduled for late the following afternoon; which Imelda thought was trashy. The reception was to be by candlelight, with a romantic "enchanted forest" theme. Imelda thought that was tacky. I heard that she hated the centerpieces, which contained bits of moss, candles, twigs, and tea-colored roses. Mandy had been crushed when she showed her the pictures and Imelda had laughed.

The next day, I was standing just outside the church door next to the groom when two limos rolled up right on time. I was about to tell Jeff to greet his parents so that I could film it. But, I stopped short at the sight of Imelda stepping out in a full-length, form-fitting navy-blue gown. She was quite stunning.

Then, just a second later, my head swiveled. The door of the other car opened and out stepped Mavis, in a full-length, form-fitting navy-blue gown. That's not something I see: mothers of the bride and the groom in matching dresses!

"Does Mandy know that both mothers are in the same dress?" I asked the groom.

"What? I thought everyone had sorted that out." Jeffrey said.

"Apparently not," I said. I shooed Jeff away when I saw the bride's limo arrive.

"You mustn't see the bride! Go and make yourself scarce!" I said.

Jeffrey's parents came inside, and soon the bridesmaids flowed into the entry of the church, nervous and giggling. Next came Mandy, then her parents came in last. Looking around, Mandy gasped.

"Look at my mother-in-law!" she said to her nearest attendant.

"Wow, she looks great! But wait, that's a blue dress!" Both women turned to look over their shoulders at Mavis who was happily chatting with the flower girls. Yup, same color, nearly the same dress.

Mandy's eyes were filled with dread as she watched her mother enter the building. When Mavis came through the door, Imelda's eyes glittered. It almost seemed like she was deciding how to play it. Would she pretend she didn't know about Mavis' dress and act violated, or would she just strut down the aisle looking hot for a sixty-year-old?

She went with outrage.

"This is an insult!" she said.

"What?" said Mavis?

"How dare you wear that dress? It was agreed! I would wear blue and you would, I don't remember, I don't care!"

Mandy's blood froze.

"Wasn't Imelda supposed to be in ivory? Didn't that piss you off because it was so close to white, but she insisted?" Mandy's bridesmaid whispered to her.

"Yeah, didn't she make a big deal about that?" another girl chimed in.

"Yes," Mandy said."Let's just get on with this."

I stepped toward the door to the sanctuary, and the wedding coordinator unconsciously put her hand on Imelda's back to move her toward the door. She refused to budge. I cringed, waiting for Imelda's reaction to being steered by the coordinator, but her focus was still on Mavis in the offending blue dress.

Then I was shocked to hear Mavis' voice.

"Listen to me. You will not hijack this day from my daughter," she said. "Either walk into that church or get out of our way, Imelda. Now!"

"You fat piece of trash, how dare you speak to me that way?" Imelda said.

Mavis stepped very close to Imelda's tall, slim body. She looked up into her face.

"Do not test me, you witch. Now I see why my daughter calls you the Dragon Lady."

"What!" Imelda seemed to be unable to breathe. "Why, that little bitch!" she said.

Turning to Mandy, she called out, "You little BITCH!" The entire bridal party froze. Mandy handed her bouquet to her best woman and moved toward the mother of the groom.

"No. Mandy, you stay there; sweetheart and you get ready to enjoy your walk down the aisle! Girls, go and check on Mandy's makeup." On cue, six young women gathered around the bride and hustled her a few yards away from the church door. They fussed and tutted over her and tried to calm her down.

Imelda was enraged, and she whirled around when Mavis grabbed her arm.

"Get your hands off of me!" she said.

"Someone go get the groom!" the coordinator said.

Finally, Bob, the father of the groom, seemed to wake up from sleep. He stepped up next to his wife and put his hand on her shoulder. "That's enough," he said.

What happened next was stunning. Imelda backed down. Glaring at Mavis, she took Bob's arm and allowed him to lead her down the aisle. The rest of the ceremony went off without a hitch.

At the reception, Imelda's running commentary got on everyone's nerves. The bride's dress didn't fit a ceremony without the Mass and Unity Candle was doomed from the start, the shrimp were spoiled, the lettuce was limp. But no one was listening and a good time was had by almost all.

Don't forget, you don't just marry your lover; you marry his or her entire family!

Approach everyone with patience, and treat them with tolerance and all will be well. If not, you can always move far away.

CHAPTER 41
PUT THE PAST BEHIND YOU

The past is not always over and done, even when a man and a woman commit to getting married. Some grooms remember the "one that got away," some brides carry torches for exes. The wedding day marks a very intentional setting aside of old loves in favor of promises of life-long fidelity. Sadly, insecurity, low self-esteem, and plain old jealousy often ruin those good intentions.

Phil, the groom disconnected his call and put his phone away.

"That was Libya," he said, referring to the matron of honor.

"What is up? Is everything okay?" Farhat, the best man asked.

"Libya said Bree plan to attend the wedding," Phil said.

"Your ex was invited?"

Farhat asked, his eyes going wide with disbelief.

"Of course not, man! Jeez. Are you crazy?" the groom said.

"OK, whew! I didn't think so!"

"You know her. That doesn't mean she won't crash," Phil said.

"Well, we'll watch for her then. We won't let her near the wedding. Fact, let me go tell the coordinator and the ushers right now."

"Good idea. Thanks," Phil said.

The best man ran to the grand foyer of the hotel to find the coordinator and the rest of the groomsmen. He explained about Bree:

"Phil has this girl that he was on and off with for years. When Phil met Jessie, well, Bree wasn't ready to let him go."

Many of the groomsmen knew the saga already. They'd been glad to see the last of Bree. They would handle her with kid gloves today, but they would relish using those gloves to throw her out.

Farhat showed the coordinator and me a photo of Bree. No need to take any chances. I left the groomsmen to find the bride and shoot her grand entrance.

Libya, the matron of honor, was just clicking off her phone when the bride came and looked over her shoulder.

"Who was that?" the bride asked.

"No one. OK, let's get you all fixed up and ready to walk down that aisle!" Libya said, pasting on a bright smile.

"What's going on?" the bride demanded.

"Nothing."

"Who were you talking to then?"

"It was Phil. I was talking to Phil."

"And why the hell would you be talking to my fiancé on the day of my wedding and not want to tell me about it?" Jessie, the bride, asked.

"God! OK, someone told me that Bree was going to come to the wedding," Libya said.

"Bree? Oh my God, that bitch!" Jessie was enraged and intimidated. I'd seen the picture. Bree was about four inches taller than the bride, and about twenty pounds lighter too. Bree had perfect skin and an air of confidence, and I overhead she'd been with Phil for years.

"Bree's crazy! There's no telling what she will do!" Jessie said.

"I know, that's why I was telling Phil. It's taken care of; everyone knows to watch for her. She probably won't even show her face!"

Libya said.

The bride, looking stricken, turned away.

"You look lovely," I said to reassure her.

"All brides do," Jessie said.

"Ah, that's not true! You are special," I said.

"There is nothing special about me," she answered.

"Your groom sees something in you!"

"What if he really still loves someone else?" she asked. I had no answer and was dumbfounded that she said such a thing out loud just moments before her walk down the aisle.

Someone smoothed her veil, and she didn't seem to notice.

When the time came for the procession, the coordinator came to gather up the bride and her attendants. One look at the bride, and she knew something was very wrong.

"Are you all right? Are you sick?" the coordinator asked.

"I'm fine," the bride said. But, there was no glow to her face, no sparkle in her voice. This was not just a case of nerves. This bride had just shut down.

"There is nothing to worry about," the coordinator said.

"What, me worry?" the bride said.

The coordinator guided the wooden bride to the door behind her attendants. Then she leaned in close to Jessie and said:

"Listen, it is up to you. You can ruin your own wedding day, or you can put a smile on your face and step out. Whatever you decide, you can't get it back."

I applauded her advice. But, I could see that the bride was slumping, fading. She was preoccupied, probably with thoughts of the beautiful Bree, radiant in a more gorgeous dress, dancing the first wedding dance in the arms of the handsome and beaming Phil.

Taking the bouquet from the coordinator, the bride walked grimly out to the hall where she would be wed. Every single attendant noticed their girl's change in mood. She had been ebullient all morning, thrilled, excited, a giddy bride. Now, she was an unsmiling robot.

I imagined a lovely woman standing up during the ceremony. She would raise her arm luxuriously when the officiant asked the question.

"If anyone knows of any reason why this man and this woman should not be wed, speak now or forever hold your peace."

I thought of how everyone in the room would turn to see Bree, to hear her say,

"I do. I am the reason."

I snapped out of my daydream and turned to the coordinator who was staring into the bride's face.

"Whatever is happening in your head isn't happening. Don't let it," she said.

The women lined up, the bride last. Instead of looking joyful, she looked like she was walking to her doom. Clearly, she had decided how the day would go.

Whether it is your wedding day or any other day, where you put your attention is what will determine your experience. Your feelings follow your thoughts. The best way not to fall victim to your insecurities is not to have any, but since everyone has them, lay them on the table with your partner, and don't marry him or her until you know you are not a rebound or a consolation prize. If he doesn't think you're the only woman on earth, don't get married thinking it'll get better once you're legal. That piece of paper won't make the insecurity, doubt, or jealousy go away. When you are sure the past is the past for your partner, let the same be true for you. Then, walk down that aisle!

CHAPTER 42
NO SEAT FOR THE WEARY

Seating arrangements are a headache. It seems as if someone always gets forgotten and has to be squeezed in at the last minute. The "singles" table always winds up a mish-mash, and though you might hope someone will hit it off and in future say they met at your wedding, it's not likely.

The hardest part of seating people is making sure there won't be any awkwardness – or outright fighting – at the table. Your friend doesn't want to sit anywhere near your cousin, but that cousin is married to your friend's brother. Your ex, who your fiancé was totally against inviting, is coming (after a bit of convincing). Even though you assure your fiancé that he is just a friend, your groom insists he sit as far away as possible from the head table. You say you'll have to give him binoculars on his way to his seat. Finally, you dis-invite him and his "plus one" because the last thing you want is a huge fight on your wedding day. It shouldn't come to that, but with alcohol on the menu, you never know.

Once you have your final guest list, ask your coordinator for a seating chart. Sit down with your fiancé and arrange the chart together so no mistakes are made.

You will be annoyed by last-minute RSVPs, especially if you have a plated dinner reception. You will write off people that don't RSVP, and just when you think you have your final guest count and you've paid your final deposit, there will inevitably be the straggling invitations in the mailbox. Do you gently tell them it's too late, or do you go back and adjust everything you've just finalized?

Of course, if someone shows up who didn't RSVP at all or who wasn't invited to your wedding – especially if they were intentionally left off the guest list -- well, then you have real problems.

During their wedding planning, Nkoli and Linus knew that there were some family members who did not get along. Linus thought he could help matters. So, he put a bright idea into motion and mixed the two families up at the dinner reception, hoping they would get to know one another and realize they actually enjoyed each other's company. Nkoli decided to let Linus try his plan, crossing her fingers that no fists would fly at her wedding. Nkoli warned me about this development and asked me very specifically to avoid filming anything disastrous. She told me she didn't want her children in years to come to see their parent's wedding turn violent.

The wedding ceremony was a huge success. I heard no complaints from anyone and I filmed happy smiles all around. I raced to the reception to capture the arrival of the guests and especially the bride and groom. It was here that things went haywire.

Discovering where they were seated, family members took it upon themselves to switch seats, moving from one corner of the hall to another, making for a very amusing game of "musical chairs" that would be great on tape. Some of the guests who believed in rules stayed right in their assigned seats, looking uncomfortable about the new arrangements. I made sure to get their expressions too.

I thought it was hysterical, as it was all done in good humor, but I could tell it was embarrassing and frustrating for Nkoli and Linus. I could appreciate Linus had good intentions, but from my experience, I could've told him people want to have some fun with their loved ones and not spend the night in awkward conversation!

When things died down, I took a break to get a Coke from the bar. I realized shortly that the seating arrangement was not going to be the issue this night. The real problem came with the very dramatic entrance of Aunt Jojo.

She was big in every way: personality, voice, volume, size. When she stepped regally into the room, her full-bodied frame filled the doorway with brilliant blue satin. The veiled and peaked hat she wore increased her already-impressive height to at least six feet. The presence of this monument of womanhood called for filming. I set down my soda. A pall came over half the wedding guests, and they stopped their chatter. It was so noticeable that the guests on the bride's side gradually hushed as well. They looked around, concerned. Their faces were priceless and didn't get missed by my video camera.

"What's the matter?" the bride's mother asked.

"LINUS!" Aunt Jojo bellowed. Now everyone was looking to the door where the majestic Aunt Jojo swayed. She seemed to be a woman in constant motion, moving shoulders and hips and chin.

She was attitude embodied. She intended to take up all the space she could. She would get the attention she deserved. She moved to the top of the stairs leading to the dance floor and dining room.

"Where is my beloved nephew?" she said.

Since everyone had quieted down and turned to stare, her booming voice was heard clearly by all. The groom, who'd been trying to duck out of the room, froze: a deer caught in the headlights. He wasn't flattered by the shot I got of him at that moment!

"Aunt Jojo," he said. He looked around desperately for his mother, Jojo's sister.

Nkoli came up beside him.

"Linus, what are we going to do? You told me that if she came, she could ruin the whole day!" Nkoli said.

"Well, nobody wants her to crash their party. She insults people. She gossips, she makes a scene…"

Linus and Nkoli were joined by Linus's mother, Celia.

"She will steal the thunder from any bride, groom, host or hostess whose rightful day it is to enjoy. Leave her to me," she said.

But before she could move, two ushers, brothers of the groom, approached Aunt Jojo. I was torn between staying to record the conversation between the bride and groom and moving toward the door to watch what would happen there. Before I could move, the two groomsmen made the mistake of taking Jojo's arms. I guess they were trying to escort her out.

Jojo took a deep breath. Her body stopped swaying. Slowly turning her head, first to the left and then to the right, she looked down at the two hands that were on her. I zoomed in on the smile that crawled over her lips. Ever-so-slowly, she raised her eyes to the men beside her.

"Oh babies, you don't want to go doing that," she said.

Pushing forward with all her weight she caught the two groomsmen off-guard, and they stumbled backward down the steps onto the dance floor. People rushed to kneel beside the two men down.

Jojo strode toward the head table where the bride's family was planning to sit. Flipping away a place card, she settled her voluptuous self-down.

"That is MY SISTER'S CHILD getting married, and I have every right to be here!" she said.

"Go ahead, *you* tell her 'no,'" I heard one of the guests say, snickering.

Aunt Jojo glared at him. She was not to be moved. The bride frantically went to accommodate her displaced guest and his wife. Seating was a mess, so she couldn't even find two seats together.

"Celia, you owe ME an apology!" Jojo said.

Celia came and sat next to her sister. I moved in close enough to hear her whisper,

"Do not do this, Sister. You had your way with Dwayne's wedding. You pulled off the veil at my wedding twenty-five years ago! I've had to keep every birthday in my family a state secret to avoid your gate-crashing!"

"Hmmmmph." Jojo said. "You have a nerve! How you don't invite your own sister to her own nephew's WEDDING! It is an insult and not to be tolerated! Now, get me the waiter. I want a wine spritzer and a cheese plate!"

Celia took that command as an excuse to get up and find the groom. I followed close behind.

"We've got to think of something. The minute she sees a microphone, she's going to be on it. The second she spots Uncle Mickey, we are all in for it!" Celia said.

I found out later that Uncle Mickey was separated from Jojo, though he didn't have the nerve to outright divorce her. He was the in-law, but he was invited. Jojo was avoided like the plague.

Nkoli started to cry. "It's my wedding day!"

"Well, she crashed, but she hasn't done anything else, really," Linus said. "Maybe we are over-reacting."

"Honey, we aren't over-anything," his mother assured him.

She turned to the bride, but Nkoli was gone.

"Where'd she go?" Celia asked, looking around.

Then she spotted her. There was Nkoli, striding purposefully toward Aunt Jojo.

Celia and Linus, panic on their faces, high-tailed it after her, both of them trying to reason with her as they went. Nkoli could be pretty formidable herself.

Nkoli stopped at Jojo's side. Too close to Jojo's side.

"We haven't met," she said, looking down at the seated woman. "I'm Nkoli. You must be Aunt Jojo. I've heard so much about you." There was the faintest threat in her voice.

Jojo looked the bride up and down, starting at the hem of her gown, examining Nkoli minutely, finally meeting the bride's eyes, unsmiling. She shoved back her chair and stood abruptly. Nkoli had no choice but to step back. She found herself looking up at Jojo, who put both hands on her wide hips and opened her mouth to speak.

"Listen, old woman," Nkoli said, speaking low so that only Jojo and a few others could hear. I moved in, not to miss anything – this was definitely highlight reel material!

"You do not want to do this. You do not want to BE on my radar because you haven't begun to know **me**. But I know a sociopath, a bully, and a bitch when I see one. You're not invited. You're never invited, not to anything. Do you know why?"

Jojo was fuming mad.

She opened her mouth, but Nkoli continued,

"Because you are this family's secret. They hide you because they are ashamed of you. They don't want you in the pictures because you ugly them up! You are a spoiled, unhappy little girl in a big woman's body! What is it with you, anyway?

Is it that your daddy loved Celia better?"

Jojo was apoplectic. It didn't look like she could even form a sentence. Nkoli began to move toward Jojo as she continued to insult, berate, scorn, threaten, and generally trash Jojo, pushing her toward the exit as she did so. And there was a smile on her face when she did it.

Before Jojo could find her tongue, her family swarmed. They pulled away Nkoli and escorted the big, brassy woman out the door. I watched them tuck her into the limo and gave the driver directions to take her home.

When I got back inside, Nkoli was smiling and chatting with her guests as if nothing had happened, the picture of innocence.

"Linus, there you are!" she said. Strange, I thought, her voice had a booming quality that sounded vaguely familiar…

How sad if you have to hide the wedding from intruding relatives! I am sure this isn't common, but learn from Linus! Don't experiment with the seating arrangements. Don't give people a reason to feel even more uncomfortable at an event where they might already not know many people. Weddings aren't the time to match-make at the singles table or to mend fences between warring family members. Seat people together because you think they will get along and if nothing else, find their dinner companions tolerable.

CHAPTER 43
THE GROOM IS ARRESTED ON HIS WEDDING DAY

I couldn't believe my eyes while I shot this scene. This story is one that made me realize I had to write this book!

Scout, Ray's two-year-old daughter was dressed up like a miniature bride to match her soon-to-be step mama, Lacy. But while Lacy was moving very little in order to keep from wrinkling, Scout was running up and down the church aisle. Lacy ignored her. She fixed her makeup in the bride's room off the vestibule in the front of the building, retouching the air-brushed perfection that was her face.

In about ten minutes, the processional would start. I blew Lacy a kiss and ran down the aisle to film the groom and his men make their entrance into the church. The groom had been ordered to stay behind the door next to the sanctuary, but when I opened it to get to him, he pulled it open wider to glare at Scout. He tried to get her attention and shook his head mouthing the word, "No!"

Scout ran up the aisle. Ray's jaw clenched. He was sweating through his tux. He had an out of control child and two groomsmen who were yet to show up. Wiping his sweaty hands on the black wool pants, Ray jumped when his best man tapped him.

"Want me to go grab her?" Craig asked.

"No, Keesha's supposed to be handling it."

"Alright, then forget about it. Relax."

Ray smiled as Lacy's mother, Tricia, came toward him. Tricia smiled coldly for the camera as she pinned on his boutonniere. She leaned in close to whisper in his ear.

"You got a problem."

"What?!" He jerked his head away from her, looking confused.

"You're a dead-beat, is that it?

I always knew something was up with you."

Ray's missing groomsmen skidded through the door, straightening themselves up as they landed. Two uniformed officers walked in right behind them. Ray looked sick. I let the camera roll. The minister opened the door while nodding to the organist to begin. Ray's head pivoted like it was on a stick.

"All set?" the minister asked Ray as the bridal march began. The minister impatiently gestured that Ray should go on into the church. Nothing could start without the groom and his men in place.

"Ray Scott?" One of the officers said.

"Yes?"

"You'll have to come with me." The cop stepped toward Ray.

"Now? I'm about to get married!"

Looking exasperated, the minister let go of the door to the sanctuary, and it swung open, letting all eighty guests see what was happening.

"Damn," said Craig, under his breath.

"We didn't know it was *your* wedding. We were just informed you would be here at this time." The officer's voice was businesslike and not especially sympathetic.

"Can you work with me here?" Ray asked.

"Sir, you haven't appeared when ordered. This action is a last resort."

"What is this about?" Craig asked.

"Unpaid child support. Eight months overdue." Tricia said.

"You haven't paid Sondra in *eight months?*" Craig got right up in Ray's face.

Ray looked away from his best man and into the church to see his baby's mama sitting on the "groom's side," right on the aisle in the first row. He looked at his soon-to-be mother-in-law.

"Sondra wasn't invited, I'm sure," Tricia said.

"No, she wasn't."

"Right, so when I saw her, I knew there was *some* reason she came. She was happy to tell me all about it*!*" Tricia said.

"She's here?" said Craig, looking past Ray. "Is that why she's here? You told me you pay her. You have Scout with you all the time! What the —"

Ray looked like he was going to vomit. His eyes darted between Tricia and Craig.

"You have to come with us. You can post bail and be out in time for your reception." The cop smirked.

"Look, officer, let me get married, and I will go with you right after. Please." Ray said.

"Yeah, maybe Lacy will understand. Good luck," Tricia said.

"Once we're married, I can fix everything. If only we could just get married?" Ray was pleading with the police officer.

"No!" Tricia interrupted. "You will not go through with this. I'm going to tell my daughter right now."

Before the officer could answer, before the mother of the bride could take another step, the entire congregation shifted in one unified motion toward the first pew where Sondra had suddenly stood up and strolled casually toward the vestibule. There, in the doorway, glittering with rage and beauty was Lacy. Clearly, she already knew everything. The room held its collective breath. Ray looked back and forth between his ex- and his almost-wife, who looked great and hot and unbelievably mad. Ray stepped through the door, into the church, moving fast toward her, arms extended and face pleading.

"Please Honey, let me…"

"No," Lacy said.

It was a voice of finality. Lacy, dangling her bouquet from its ribbon, turned elegantly and walked out of the church.

The police officers followed Ray up the aisle as the organist abruptly stopped playing. A stunned silence held everyone in the room captive. Only Scout could be heard from the vestibule, asking her mama for something to drink.

The best man stepped to the front of the church as Ray and the officers followed Lacy out the front doors. I paused, unsure if I should follow her, but then I heard the best man:

"Ladies and gentlemen, there has been a bit of a situation. If I could ask for your patience, I am sure this will all be straightened out. Thank you!" Craig said.

The minister and Craig held a quick conference and then Craig ran to catch up with the groom and his escorts. The minister spoke to the musician, and the organ started playing again. The guests buzzed, speculating and gossiping.

An hour later, everybody had abandoned their pews, the minister had left, and organist had long since packed up his organ shoes and gone home. I didn't know what to do, so I stood around with members of the wedding party, texting and wondering what would happen next. When the best man, Craig, pulled up, the groomsmen were drinking the champagne from the limo. Craig told them what had happened at the precinct.

"We can bail him out if we can come up with $18, 000," Craig said.

"How are we going to do that?" Sean asked.

"We're his ushers; we've got to come up with something,"

Craig said.

"We have to ask the guests," Sean said.

"Right." Craig waved his arms to get everyone's attention. "Can we all go inside for a minute? Hey! Excuse me! Can you come with me, just come inside for a minute, and I can tell you what's happening."

After ten minutes, all the guests who'd stayed around were corralled back into the church. Craig stood up front and explained that this being Saturday, unless they could come up with $18,000, the groom would be spending the weekend in jail.

"Where's Lacy?" someone called out.

"She's with Ray, at the police station," Craig answered.

"Yeah, she's dressed for it!" somebody joked.

"Listen, they can get married at the catering hall later, but we have to get out of here, and we have to bail Ray out. Who's with me?"

"Lacy still wants to marry him?" someone asked.

"The wedding's on?"

"Yes, they are still going to get married. Ray is really sorry. He just got behind on some child support, that's it. He's not a criminal or anything!" Craig said.

"Not supporting his kid *is* criminal. I'm out of here," a friend of Lucy's said, and when she stood up to leave, two others went with her.

"OK, OK, who can help us out here? You all were bringing wedding presents, cash, money, right? What if we started with that?" Craig said.

"Right. Open up your envelopes and I'll come and collect it and see where we're at," Sean said.

On the first pass, the wedding guests were able to raise $2400.

"That's not going to cut it, people," Craig said. He went over to Ray's father and mother and had a few words with them. Then he came back to the front of the sanctuary.

"OK, Ray's parents will come up with $5000, we have $2400. I am asking for a loan here. I'll sign the note myself. We'll keep track of where the money comes from," Craig said.

"Who is willing to take a ride to the ATM machine and meet up at the catering hall?" Sean said. A few people raised their hands, and a cheer went up. The reception was paid for and Craig made it clear that no matter what else happened, everyone was invited to Everknot Manor for dinner.

By seven o'clock, I was at Everknot, Ray had been in jail for three hours, Lacy was nowhere to be seen, and most of the guests had trickled into the reception where the cocktail hour had been stretched out as long as it could go.

Craig and Sean stayed at the entrance, sipping their cocktails and cajoling guests for additional donations to bail out the groom. As the finger foods and drinks smoothed out the tangles of the day, people started having fun. Pocketbooks were opened wider, and relatives became more and more generous as the evening wore on.

"I can't let the groom miss his wedding day," Ray's uncle said.

The DJ kept the music going, and the MC encouraged everyone to get up and dance. At first, people hesitated, but he said,

"Nothing you can do folks, except enjoy your night. You're all dressed up for nothing? No! Come out and dance! Wedding party – it's your party now! Show your guests what they should do!"

Finally, around 8 pm, Craig grabbed the microphone and announced that he had enough money to bail Ray out. Cheers went up. The music came back on, the waiters started taking dinner orders, and the wedding party went up to the bridal suite to get ready for a wedding ceremony.

It was nearly 10 pm by the time Ray was processed and released. As soon as he got to the hall, the DJ took over, telling everyone to take a seat, putting on music for the procession.

The wedding party entered in pairs, loose and laughing, looking relieved after a long stressful day. Finally, there was Ray with the bride on his arm. Together, they took the long walk down the aisle. Not the church wedding they had planned for, but it was a beautiful ceremony, followed by a very late but delicious dinner.

Truth be told, a good time was had by all.

No one should have to deal with this kind of drama on their wedding day. But, as they say, "a woman scorned" is the worst sort enemy to have. Was the motive of this baby mama to get the groom's attention, to make the point that she was very serious about their financial arrangement, or did she want the whole world to think that he is a bad father? Of course, some people can be cold evil, undermining the relationship between father and daughter, or causing resentment with family members. This baby mama wanted to embarrass the groom on his wedding day, and she succeeded!

You might say the groom was a dead-beat dad and deserved what he got. Of course, the child comes first.

Before you decide to get married, get that part of your house in order to give your kids the best foundation you can.

CHAPTER 44
SAYING TOO MUCH

Too many wedding speeches (or toasts) go horribly wrong. Uncle Tom gets drunk and over-shares about your bachelor party. Best friend, Mindy, starts out sweet and touching and then veers off into the painful and embarrassing. Some are "all in good fun," others are just in bad taste. What your 30-year-old aunt may find funny, your 95-year-old grandmother may not, or the other way around. There are speeches that turn into crying jags and some that last (for what seems like) hours.

Choose your speech-maker wisely. Have a little pre-speech talk with him or her. Politely ask them to keep it short – they will be relieved, and your guests will thank you. If you don't want to get emotional, ask them to keep it light. If you don't want them to get too personal, ask them to keep it general. It's all about reminiscing about the past and wishing you the best for the future. They will be glad for the guidelines.

Janet wasn't very happy when her fiancé Dan invited his ex-girlfriend Candy to their wedding. I thought Janet was crazy to agree to it. The way she looked at him, it was obvious that Candy still carried a torch for Dan and if any opportunity arose for her to make a move, she'd take it.

Janet spoke to Dan warning him to stay out of dark corners during the reception.

"I won't leave your side, Baby," he said.

After watching her for a while, I thought maybe I'd read it wrong. Maybe Candy wasn't trying to seduce Dan. She wanted to reminisce and spend the time gazing at him with love rather than lust. She was clearly still pining for him. The thing that worried me was that she was getting drunk as the night wore on.

"Um. Janet? You might want to say something to Dan," the bride's friend said at around 9 pm.

Janet had been chatting with relatives from the other coast, and she looked up, scanning the room for something amiss.

"Why?" Janet asked.

"Candy wants to make a speech. And she's loaded."

"No one is going to let her do that!" Janet said.

"Look over there."

Janet looked just in time to see the DJ handing Candy a microphone.

"NO," she said. "Where's Dan?"

It was too late. The music had stopped, and Candy was tapping the microphone and asking for everyone's attention. It was clear right off that she was in no condition to give a speech. Her voice broke as she gave what sounded like an eulogy for Dan. He stood, paralyzed and red-faced through it all.

The best man, doing his duty, gently tried wrenching the microphone out of Candy's hand in order to escort her out, but she became even more emotional and determined.

"Dan, you are one in a million, and I'm an idiot for letting you go," she said.

We could all see Dan sweat.

"I'll never forget the night you told me about Janet – I think you'd been going out for about a month by then…"

"WHAT?" Janet said, looking at Dan. "You were still seeing her?" She walked toward the DJ booth as Candy continued,

"It was late, and I was a little tipsy – like now," she said, giggling. "You got up to get dressed and –"

"WHAT?" Janet screamed.

"Uh oh," Candy said as Dan grabbed her arm and marched her away from his new bride.

When Janet stormed after them, I heard Uncle Milt say, "I guess there won't be any cake."

It was a dramatic exit, but Dan smoothed it all over with Janet, assuring her that Candy was just drunk. But still, it was a scene that could have been avoided with more attention to that guest list and oversight by the DJ. Have your toasts early, before too much alcohol is consumed. Give the DJ a list of who will be speaking, and never let him offer an "open mic."

CHAPTER 45
CRY BABY

My friend who is a minister conducted premarital preparation with this couple and shared the story with me. Although the wedding had some hiccups, husband and wife shared many happy years together.

Bob had been married twice, and his second divorce had been particularly bitter. Bob had women friends but swore up and down that he would never get married again. That is until he met Barbie.

Barbie was widowed and actively searching for someone to connect with at a deep level. She was a businesswoman who went home to a lonely house every night and longed for companionship, though she didn't think she'd ever find a man like her husband, Don. He was one in a million – generous, kind, supportive and sexy. She missed him every day.

Bob decided that the pool of dating prospects was too shallow in the small town where he lived, so he went on a few dating websites and browsed. After a couple of weeks, he took the plunge and paid for a subscription to a promising site. Bob posted a profile – using a picture from about ten years before. Bob haunted that site night after night, not even sure what he was expecting or what he was looking for. Until he saw a profile of a woman named Barbie.

Barbie was dark-eyed and raven-haired. She had aged gracefully and had maintained a lovely figure and a bright smile. She posted her absolute best photo, and though she was dissatisfied with it, she hoped that the right man would see more than her face and body – that he would be looking for a deeper connection than the physical.

When Bob and Barbie connected online, the commonalities and synchronicities of their lives stunned them. Their experiences, wants, hopes – it all seemed to spark. They very quickly decided to meet. They hit it off immediately, an instant attraction. Both laughingly admitted to using Photoshop and ancient pictures to look their best on the dating site. Within a very short time, they were both telling everyone about their "second chance" and how neither of them believed that at the advanced ages of "50-plus" they could find such a love again.

They decided to get married and found my friend's "cute church." They planned a simple wedding and decided to ask all of their adult children to stand up for them. Then, at their engagement party at Barbie's daughter's house, in a moment of too much wine and enthusiasm,

Bob said,

"I am thrilled our families get along so well, and I'm so happy that you kids agreed to be in our wedding party. I think it would be great for all the grandkids to stand up with us as well!"

"Bob, I don't know…" Barbie said.

"Sure. It'll be great!" Bob said.

The grandchildren – eight of them – ranged in age from 12 months to 8 years. Barbie figured there was no need to worry about the 7 and 8-year-olds, but the babies, well, they were another matter. She knew that Bob was not particularly patient with his grandkids, and he barely knew hers.

Barbie was reluctant to upset Bob, and she knew that when his enthusiasm flared, when his generosity outweighed his bank account, or his exuberance overcame his common sense, she should ride along and enjoy it.

Bob was not a calm man. His face flushed bright red at the first sign of frustration. He had a temper and not a lot of patience. He often spoke and acted without much forethought and then had to deal with the consequences. This would turn out to be one of those occasions.

At the rehearsal, the minister counseled the couple to let the children walk down the aisle (if they must), and then sit with babysitters or relatives who weren't in the wedding party.

"Someone they trust and will go to -- who won't be heartbroken to miss the ceremony. Not a parent. Someone willing to grab and go – get the child out if he starts to cry," the minister said. "Their parents won't be able to leave the altar and the littlest ones are going to see mommy or daddy and want to be with them."

"The kids are going to be up there with their parents. Everyone is standing up with us," Bob said. The minister could tell his confidence in this plan was wavering by the tone of his voice and the way his eyes shifted when he said it. He was watching the children running rampant around the sanctuary at that very moment -- getting very comfortable with this setting so that they could run rampant during the wedding too.

"Well, these little guys, they might not be able to stand still during a twenty-minute ceremony," the minister said.

"Bob, I think he might be right…" Barbie said.

"Let's go ahead," Bob said.

"You kids can keep the children quiet, right?"

The parents all nodded their heads, looking at their little darlings pulling the cushions off the pews and running up and down all over the balcony stairs.

On the morning of the wedding, having gotten dressed at his daughter's house, Bob was soon frustrated with the three grandchildren who lived there. His reddened neck strained against the too-tight collar of his tuxedo shirt, and he was perspiring conspicuously.

"Jeez, Becky, is this how they are in the morning?"

"Dad, this is how they are all day," Becky said.

"Mommy!!!" wailed little Mickey.

"Ow! Stop it!" the twins said in unison.

"Let's get in the limo and get to the church," Bob said. So they did.

The children and grandchildren all lined up peacefully in the narthex. The bride smiled beautifully behind the entourage while Bob waited with his eldest son in the sanctuary. The minister relaxed, thinking that maybe it would go according to plan after all. But children could be such a wild card – and here were eight of them.

The Wedding March began and everyone filed up the aisle in perfect formation, each taking their place on the white dots the minister had stuck to the floor of the altar. The only hitch was when little Mira dropped her flowers and ran to her daddy, the best man, crying all the way. The congregation laughed indulgently. But Bob said, through gritted teeth,

"Why is she crying?"

His son just shrugged as he picked up his daughter.

"Dearly beloved," the minister began, once everyone was in place.

"MINE!" said little Deirdre, grabbing her cousin's bouquet.

"NO! Give it!" said 3-year-old Susie, defending her flowers.

"Shhhhh," whispered both mommies simultaneously.

Peace was restored. Bob reset his smile, nodded at the minister, who began once again.

"Dear Friends, we are gathered…"

Mira, still in her father's arms after her mishap with the flowers, decided it was time to have a little chat. Toying with his boutonniere, she began a monologue about her favorite cartoon. Bob glared and gave a small shake of his head to Mira's dad.

Everyone else, including the minister, tried to ignore the disruption. Just then, the cousins competing over the flowers sat down and began to take apart their beautiful bouquets, trading flowers back and forth, chattering about sharing.

Bob glanced down at the two little angels and smiled tightly. Mira, by this time, had stopped chatting and had begun to point and cry. She wanted to trade flowers too. One of the daddies tried to reason with the girls, making even more noise. Barbie's smile never budged, but her eyes were glued to the groom's face, which was growing ever redder, anger spreading like a five-alarm fire.

At this point, all of the under-fives were chatting or crying at various volumes, each spurred on by the others. The minister had no choice but to stop talking altogether. It was chaos, the worst he had ever seen. For once, he was speechless and had no idea how to regain control over the room. He could feel sweat drip down his back into the waistband of his pants.

Sweating profusely himself, Bob seethed. Barbie held her breath. The entire congregation looked on, barely breathing themselves, waiting for what would happen next. The tension was painful, and several guests were shifting in their seats and looking at the exits.

"Take them out." Bob said. Everyone could hear, though Bob meant it to be a whisper. The congregation gasped.

At first, no one moved.

"I said, take them out!" He said.

It wasn't until Barbie nodded at the lot of them that they all grabbed their children and headed for the side door into the hall, far enough away that Bob could marry his bride undisturbed.

The only two people remaining on the altar with the couple were the seven and eight-year-old grandchildren.

In the hall, Bob and Barbie's kids dreaded the receiving line and wondered what sort of apology would be enough to soothe Bob's temper.

In the sanctuary, Bob smiled and took a deep breath. Today, he would marry his beloved, his partner in life, his true love – and nothing would take his joy from him.

It is commendable to want your beloved family to gather around you on your wedding day, but perhaps the church isn't the best place to demonstrate your togetherness. There are people who don't even invite children to their weddings to avoid the disruption they can cause. There are parents who wouldn't dream of leaving their little ones at home and others who would be grateful for a break. Be clear, parents and grandparents, children under 7 or 8 are unpredictable at best. Outfit them with a handler, show that person where all the exits are, and instruct them to remove the child when they get antsy. Worry about offending the parents of those little noise makers later. This is your wedding, and you have every right to enjoy it uninterrupted.

CHAPTER 46
KNOW WHEN TO SHUT UP

A good DJ can help move your reception program along, but be clear on the bells and whistles. Not every wedding needs neon bracelets and endless encouragement to "shake what your mama gave you."

The DJ can introduce the wedding party, keep a flow of music appropriate for cocktail hour, dinner, and dancing. He or she announces the first dance, the cutting of the cake, the garter, and the tossing of the bouquet, but a DJ can be impersonal. Aside from going over a playlist, how much time do you spend with your DJ before the ceremony? Be clear about the types of music and antics that are permissible. Your crowd might be too conservative for the Chicken Dance, they might prefer country line dancing, might feel forced out of the room by volume that is TOO HIGH. Tell your DJ your concerns.

Some couples hire or recruit a Master of Ceremonies – MC. Best would be the MC that knows the bride and groom intimately. This way, you avoid the awkward mispronunciation of names, jokes that offend, and the fake, over-enthusiastic and over-used tropes of most DJs: "Hey! Give the happy couple a hand."

The DJ or MC that sounds like a game show host is the worst cliché. Go and hear your potentials perform so you can be sure you're getting a performance that suits *you*. The voice and music that rules the night can make or break your reception. Discourage the "one man shows."

The minute the DJ veers off into his own territory – stop him. Tell him in no uncertain terms what you want and don't want, right there on the spot.

Send the best man if you wish, or better yet, send whoever is paying for him: father of the bride, perhaps?

If you have a friend in mind to serve as your MC, have a gift ready for him or her, or pay them outright. They might hand the cash right back to you, but you'll show appreciation by the offer. If you worry you might offend them, suggest they give the money to charity if they'd prefer, or tell them, "It's our wedding gift to you for the gift you've given us!"

At our first meeting, Stuart and Malini told me they'd invited their close friend Stephanie to host their wedding reception. It wasn't common, but I'd seen people have friends or relatives serve as an MC before. I was a little apprehensive, and I told them so.

"I've videotaped a lot of weddings, and the best ones that flow the smoothest, without a hitch -- those don't rely on amateurs," I said.

"Stephanie's a teacher; she's in front of a classroom all the time. She's the Union Rep for her district, and she gives talks to rooms full of hostile people. She will do great," Malini said.

"And, she's really funny. Witty, you know? Always quick on her feet with a come- back, especially after a few pops," Stuart said.

"My friends, really, you might be right, but drinking and MCing a wedding are a bad combination. That's why we professionals don't drink at weddings. We've got a job to do," I said.

"Well, she's a guest, and it's not her job," Malini said.

Sensing I was about to offend them, I cut it off. I would hope for the best and have the camera ready for the disaster I predicted.

Malini and Stuart said they'd been clear with Stephanie that when music was on, she could just enjoy herself; eat, drink, and dance. They had asked her to be the "glue" for the rest of it, introducing the wedding party, calling for the three important dances with mother, father, and couples first. She also would MC a slide show that took the guests through a retrospective of the couple's life, from their childhood up until their meeting, courtship, wedding planning, and wedding day. Stephanie agreed to take some shots of the ceremony and add them into the presentation in the short time-frame between church and catering hall.

In addition to the traditional announcements, Stephanie promised a "surprise."Caught up in the excitement of a great meeting where they had all enthusiastically agreed on scripts, photos, and the order of the night, the couple had agreed, thrilled and touched that she wanted to go that extra mile to make the reception special.

On the night of the wedding, Stephanie masterfully announced the wedding party, ushering them into the venue to the DJ's pounding music and flashing lights. The crowd cheered, and from behind the entourage, the couple looked at each other and smiled.

"She's going to be good!"

Malini said, and Stuart nodded in agreement.

The newlyweds were announced and went immediately into their first dance. The music slowed and quieted, the lights dimmed. The wedding party ringed the dance floor, smiling as the couple came together in a sweet, slow, traditional foxtrot they had learned just for this moment.

I was thrilled with the shots of tearful expressions, and a room full of people captivated by the bride and groom, perfectly decked out and dancing beautifully. All of a sudden, we were all startled by a strange narration that began,

"There they are, folks, a little sweaty because of nerves, but looking extremely great!"

Malini lifted her head from Stuart's shoulder and frowned at him. He looked around to find Stephanie.

"Yep, they rehearsed this dance for months! Stuart needed the time, considering his two left feet!"

A couple of people snickered. Others looked uncomfortable. I didn't know what to film – the crowd as it started to get nervous, the crazy MC, or the couple on the dance floor.

"Now you can get a good look at the $10,000 dress! You can judge for yourself whether the cummerbund matches the bridesmaid dresses!"

"What is she doing?" Malini said.

"Oops, guys! One-two-three-four, One-two-three-four! It's a foxtrot, not the Lindy!"Stephanie laughed loudly and gestured for the crowd to do the same.

A few people laughed limply. I zoomed in on Stephanie's face and could clearly see that she was rapidly on her way to smashed.

The DJ took over and moved into the next song, which was a faster tempo, and the wedding party took their cue and got on the floor with the bride and groom. I couldn't see their faces anymore, so I resumed my normal taping at this point. Shortly, I had a chance to catch the couple smiling again, dancing with their flower girl and junior bridesmaid.

Before long, Stephanie announced dinner and people took their seats. This was usually a time when speeches could be made or other ceremonial events could happen. Waiters were discretely taking dinner orders, and at the far end of the hall, salad plates were coming out.

"So, we want to welcome you to Malini and Stuart's wedding!" Stephanie said and the guests all applauded and cheered.

"Would you guys stand up for the best man's toast?" Stephanie said. She turned to Ron, who was getting up to take the microphone.

"OK. Here's your chance. Don't muck it up," she said, handing him the microphone.

I moved in close for this exchange. Ron's jaw clenched, but he forced a smile and did his speech. The bride and groom had heard the comment from their MC, and their faces were stiff and plastered with smiles. Their expressions didn't change when Ron was finished and came to kiss them. Neither did they change when their maid of honor was called out for her own words.

Stephanie didn't make any comments but tried to fake Sammy out by pulling back the microphone as she reached for it three times. Finally, she handed it over with a shrug and a funny face to the crowd. I could see her reach for her drink as she stood back for Sammy to pass.

Stephanie didn't say anything after the maid of honor's words so everyone awkwardly began to eat and chat again. In the silence, the DJ jiggled his headphones waiting for his cue. Finally, he decided to go on with the dinner music.

About halfway through dinner, Stephanie stood up unsteadily. I dropped my fork and grabbed my camera, rushing to get in front of her. She didn't seem to notice me, and I was glad about that.

"Now, there is this show I want to show you," she said,

"Hey that rhymes!"

The lights went down, and a PowerPoint presentation began. People oohed and aahed over the baby pictures, and laughed gently at the gawky pictures of Malini and Stuart as pre-teens and adolescents. Stephanie didn't make any comments, and I saw Malini shrug when Stuart whispered something to her. My guess was there was a script and Stephanie wasn't on it.

She sped through the PowerPoint to the last few slides – the ones of the ceremony that she had tacked onto the end of the show the couple had taken weeks to assemble.

The first shot was of Malini rubbing her nose in the narthex before she walked down the aisle. Stephanie laughed out loud. Next was a shot of Malini making a terrible face at the misbehaving flower girl. She looked like a hissing snake, and nothing like the composed and gracious bride she wanted to be. After these two humiliating photos came shots from the worst possible angles, creating bellies, double chins, dark under-eye bags, and every other imperfection possible on the faces and bodies of a lovely bride and handsome groom. Malini was near tears by the end of the show. Stephanie was doubled over in laughter, oblivious to the silence of the entire room.

She narrated the last slide,

"Happily ever after! It only gets uglier from here kids. So drink up!" She held up her glass and invited the couple to toast with her. When they didn't, her eyes hardened.

"OK, then. Let's get to my surprise! I don't want to give it away, but it's a trivia game!"

Malini covered her mouth with her hand. Stuart stood up, ready to walk over to Stephanie.

"First question. When was the first time Malini and Stu hooked up? Hint: it wasn't when their ex's thought it was!" Stephanie said.

From there, the room was a melee, and the father of the bride quickly strode toward Stephanie and removed the microphone from her hand. She battled for it, then gave it up, laughing and grabbing her large glass of what could've been water but I'd bet was vodka.

The DJ came over the sound system inviting everyone to dance and played what he remembered was the bride's favorite song. From that moment, he was in charge and "Wedding Moves by Dave" saved the day. The groom tipped Dave heavily at the end of the night. He deserved it.

Choose your MC wisely. You might love Uncle Stan and find him charming at holiday gatherings but how is he in front of a crowd? Be sure his comments will include both the bride's and groom's side. Avoid jokes and memories that come from one holiday table only. Share stories, and have your MC talk to your wedding party and family – particularly if he or she is going to narrate a PowerPoint show of your childhoods, courtship, families and the like.

As a professional who has seen things go wrong, my advice:

Hire a good MC.

CHAPTER 47
LAST-MINUTE BLITZ

There are people who start their planning two years in advance and others who procrastinate, assuming there is plenty of time. Some folks focus so intently on one aspect of the wedding day (the dress, maybe?) that the rest takes a back seat.

Putting things off doesn't only make it harder to get the vendors you want (they book up months in advance). It doesn't only stress out your partner (they might be a procrastinator too, or not really care too much whether the band, the cake, the caterer are last-minute choices, the only ones available at short notice). It doesn't only give your mother fits. Putting things off removes any chance that you will enjoy the last few weeks leading up to your wedding. Instead of calmly opening cards and gifts, celebrating at engagement parties, brunches, and a rehearsal dinner, you will be scrambling.

The Do-It-Yourself bride or groom is going to be most taxed on the wedding morning if they have put things off. Even if they are on-task, the checklist of last-minute details can mean you have to forgo the manicure, the shave, and finishing touches that would make things extra-special.

For example, Mary, who'd wanted a small backyard wedding returned home after getting her nails done and had stopped short looking at her lawn, seeing it as if for the first time. She couldn't have forty people standing on this patchy grass!

She ran out to Home Depot where she had seen piles of sod laid out just the day before. Opening the back of her Trooper, she loaded sheet after sheet of sod and sped home. For the next seven hours, she installed sod, pausing only to give her out-of-town parents some dinner. Even after it started to pour down rain, she put in her sod. By 11 pm, the sod looked lovely, being watered in by a huge storm, but her nails were ruined, and she was exhausted. She'd enlisted her 70-year-old mother to help her, and she had to tuck her into a warm bath because the woman was chilled to the bone from planting sod in the cold spring rain.

The lawn looked great for the wedding the next day, and her husband couldn't believe his crazy new wife.

Another backyard bride whose story I am privy to is Delia. She was an average mix of procrastinator and checklist girl. She knew people who were far worse, so she thought of herself as fairly prompt and organized. Delia and max had invited 100 guests to attend their wedding in her parents' big backyard. There would be a tent for dinner, an arch to get married under. There'd be rows of white chairs set up for the ceremony, which would be moved around the tables for the dinner. The landscaping had to be worked on, and the pool would be open for the late-night partiers who might want a swim. The caterer was using her kitchen but bringing in a lot of cold platters to make things easier.

Delia's friends suggested she get a helping hand, but she believed the caterer would be help enough. She arranged the minister, the DJ and the photographer; she just trusted they'd show up on time and do what they had to do. She had baked the cake herself and though she still had to finish the fondant, she was pretty confident she would get it all done.

Max, her fiancé, was a busy florist and ran around to such events for a living. He tacked his own wedding delivery to the others scheduled for the morning of the wedding.

The first sign of trouble occurred at 7 am when the bride overslept. She bounded from her bed furious that Max hadn't woken her when he'd gotten up at six.

She ran to the kitchen, making coffee, taking plastic off her dress, putting soda cans into coolers and preparing the fondant for the cake.

She glanced up at the clock at ten and felt her heart race. Glancing at her reflection in the window over the sink, she decided that laying out the rest of the stemware would have to wait. As she ran upstairs to shower, the doorbell rang, and she was glad to see the caterer's girl at the door. She put her to work laying out tableware in the dining area outside. Fortunately, the day was perfect, dry and warm.

Delia showered and rolled her hair to obtain that perfect, glossy wave she desired. While she was setting her hair, her best woman came in and offered to help. Delia resisted, but glancing at the clock, she agreed it was time to send in the troops. Delia quickly jotted down a list of things that still had to be done.

"Amy, can you get Luke to pick up the tux?"

Amy started her own list. "Yup. What else?"

"Check on the girl outside. She has to set the tables with the silverware linens folded the way I showed her. I left her a sample, plus wine glasses and champagne flutes at each seat."

"I'll check," Amy replied.

"Ice, Jeez! Ask Jeff to pick up ice and see that the coolers are all filled. Also, put some more soda into the coolers that are outside. I did the beer, but I got side-tracked."

"Got it."

"Oh! My God! My nails!" Delia said.

"OK, sit down, I'll paint them for you, just relax. Let me go down and check on the girl and call Jeff about the ice and Luke about the tux."

"Oh! My God! Tell Jeff, also the bread! I said I'd pick it up at six from the Italian bakery! I totally forgot."

Delia was hyperventilating.

"Check!"

"And where the hell is Max? He said he'd only need to do deliveries until noon! Honestly, why he couldn't delegate that and be here with me!"

"Well, delegating isn't anybody's strong suit around here, hmmmm?" Amy said.

Delia sat to do her makeup, and Amy ran to cover her bases. She was back shortly and sat Delia down to relax her and do her nails. She tried to calm down with a small glass of white wine.

The minute Amy proclaimed the nails done, Delia jumped up to head back to the kitchen.

"Wait till they dry! It's only 1 pm, you're OK!" Amy said.

But Delia had a million things on her mind: she wanted to see if the caterer's girl was on-task. She wanted to get that cake decorated and had to be sure that the caterer was planning to arrive at two as she'd said.

Walking down the stairs, talking on the phone, and blowing on her nails, the unthinkable happened. Delia fell down the stairs, twisting her ankle painfully.

"Ow!!!"

Amy came running to the head of the stairs and raced down to her dear friend.

"Don't move! Is anything broken? Did you hit your head?"

"No, I don't think so. But my ankle – I'm not sure I can stand on it," Delia said.

They got her to the couch, and Amy propped up her foot. She looked around to see that the room seriously needed to be picked up before guests started arriving in a few hours. She knew they were supposed to go around back, but inevitably some people who thought they were special would come in through the front door and expect to be welcome.

"I'm getting you ice, then I'm cleaning up this room and the dining room too."

"Be careful of the cake! The cake is on the table!" Delia said.

Amy went into the kitchen through the dining room straightening up as she went. When she passed the cake, she gasped. She'd heard a lot about the cake. Delia had made a few of her nieces' birthday cakes, but everyone had told her that she shouldn't attempt a wedding cake, especially her own. Here was the cake with half-done fondant icing, (oddly colorful for a wedding cake,) melting in the warmth of sunlight streaming through the dining room window. Colors were running down the sides, smeared and blurring what she assumed was supposed to be a rainbow. With a muttered curse, Amy ran to get a bag of ice.

"Dee, there's something you should know about the cake," Amy said once Delia had Advil and ice.

"Don't tell me!" Delia said.

"OK, um, I think we better come up with a plan B. Where's Max?" Amy said.

"I just texted him about my ankle. He'll be here."

Just a few minutes later, Max raced into the house and knelt by Delia. By this time, it was 2 pm, and the caterer was setting up in the kitchen. The room was virtually impassable with her utensils, equipment, trays of food, and two helpers. Amy was frantically finishing the quick-clean of the downstairs. She'd found the bathroom had yet to be touched, so she handled that too. She'd only paused a moment to console a crying and frantic Delia who had finally looked at a picture of the cake on Amy's phone. It was bad.

Max wasn't given any time to be attentive.

"Go to the bakery, any bakery and get a cake! A sheet cake, an ice cream cake, cupcakes- I don't care! Enough for everyone."

"Um, how many people did we invite?" Max asked.

"Oh, my God!"

Max left before the bride could throw something, passing his best man on the way in with the tuxes, right behind Jeff bringing in the bread and ice.

"Can't talk," he said. "Grab a beer and get dressed in the upstairs guest room!" And he was off.

The rest of the wedding party trickled in, and the women helped Delia back upstairs to get dressed. All the rest of the tasks she wanted to lovingly do had to be left to others. She had seen herself as Martha Stewart on the cover of her Gracious Entertaining book – head cocked to one side with a calm smile on her face as she prepared Duck L'orange for three hundred -- on hand thrown plates with stemware delivered just that morning and adorned with roses and raspberries moments before. But Delia wasn't Martha, and it was not to be. But, it was for the best, as guests came dressed more casually than she had thought they would. To them, it was a backyard wedding and no need for formality. That was probably what saved the day. When she hobbled up the aisle to a cheering crowd, Delia burst into tears of joy – and relief.

Delegate! It's the secret to everyone's success – even Martha Stewart!

CHAPTER 48
HAIR AND THERE

They say your hair is your crowning glory. Well, give it the time and attention it deserves then! Don't rush your hair appointments, experiment wildly in the weeks leading up to your wedding, but not on the day of the wedding. Let your girls get their hair done with their own hairdresser if they will feel more comfortable. And most important, make it very clear who will be paying for the stylists, hairdressers, and cosmetologists.

This story was told to me in hilarious detail by the best woman. I saw the tension on all the girls' faces when I met them before the wedding.

"Marilee is the best! You will love her!" Misha announced.

"OK, are we going to see her for try-outs, you know, to see how we want our hair?" Tamika asked.

"I want you all to look the same. You all get the same hairstyle." Misha said.

"Mish, none of our hair is the same, girl!" Tamika said.

"Nobody's going to look the same! Look at our bodies!" Rhonda said. All the girls laughed at that, looking around at big bottoms and small waists, long legs and short ones. This wasn't a matching group.

"Mish, you tried that with the dresses! Remember you had to give up on the spaghetti straps for Ro because of the size of her boobs? And you had to do the wrap around thing for Tamika because she's like ten months pregnant already!"

"I remember," Misha said.

"So, let's go get a spa day and let this chick do our hair!" Tamika said.

"It'll cost all of you money to do that!" Misha said.

"True. Ok, so how many girls is she bringing?

There's six of us, plus you."

"Well, I'm going first!" Misha said and everyone laughed.

"Sure, sure," said Ro. "How many girls? And are they doing our nails, too?"

"Only Marilee. She's all we're going to need. Trust me."

"Whoa, whoa! Misha,

What time is she going to start us? 4 am?" Ro asked.

"Around six." Misha said.

"You are dam right you are going first. Call me to come over around 10," Tamika said.

Everybody laughed and agreed they wanted to be called when the girl ahead of them was finished so they could get their beauty sleep.

"We have to go to her salon. Her private one in her basement," Misha said.

"Where's that?" Ro asked.

"Harriman."

"Mish, that's like a half hour from here! Then we're coming back here to get dressed?"

"Is she doing our makeup too? Nails? What?" Ro asked.

"Just hair," Misha said. She was feeling defensive. "You can all get your nails done the day before."

"We can do each other's makeup!" Ro said. "That'll be fun. We'll play 'beauty parlor' like when we were in school!"

"Well, Marilee is going to do my makeup," Misha said.

"Of course she is! You're the bride," Ro said, but everyone went quiet. There were some doubts about getting everyone done in a few hours. Plus, they'd have to leave time for travel, getting dressed, and made up in time to get picked up and brought to the church by 4 pm. It didn't leave a whole lot of wiggle room.

On the day of the wedding, Misha was up at 4:00, unable to sleep and completely stressed about the hairdresser. What if she couldn't get everyone done in time?

At six, nobody was at her house yet for the drive to Harriman. She called Marilee.

"Hi, Marilee, I guess we will be a little late. No one is here yet, and we are all supposed to drive together."

"Hi Misha! Well, two of your girls are here already, so I got started on them. Rhonda and Leena? We're getting them under the dryer now."

"What? How did you set their hair? What time did they get there? It's only six-thirty!"

"Relax, I started with a wash and set, and we'll get them dry, and by the time you get here, you can give me input on styling."

Misha was furious that Ro and Leena had gone ahead without her. They would be made to pay for the disrespect they were showing her.

Finally, at 7 am, the rest of the bridal party arrived, and they set out to Marilee's house in Harriman. Everyone insisted on a stop at Starbucks before going too far. Misha was getting nervous about the time. At least two girls would be almost done by the time she got there, she reasoned. Plus, those two could get out of her sight and head home to dress and do each other's faces alone.

Misha barely looked at Ro and Leena. Marilee had done a beautiful job on the both of them but neither looked anything like Misha had wanted, and they definitely didn't look the same.

"What's this? Where's the up-do? Where's the whole fancy French bun thing?" she said.

"Misha, I was planning on that with you, like we talked about. You wanted everybody to have that look? Don't these styles work great for Rhonda and Leena?" Marilee asked.

The women looked gorgeous – even without makeup. They giggled and looked at themselves in the mirror from all angles.

Misha decided it wasn't worth the aggravation, and it was already eight o'clock.

"Whatever. Now, why don't you two B—s pay the lady and get on your way?"

"Who's paying?" Rhonda said.

"You are – everybody is!" Misha said, "Did you think I was paying to have everyone's hair done?"

"I'd have gone to my girl in that case! I have a credit with her!" Rhonda said.

"Oh my God, you have GOT to be kidding me!" Misha said.

"How much is it Marilee?" Leena asked.

"Well, it's a Saturday, but your guys didn't get a big elaborate up-do. So, $40. 00."

"I can do $35. 00," Leena said.

"Um, Misha, this isn't what I do!" Marilee said. She had no plan to negotiate on her price. Up-dos were more, and $40 was a fair price for the styles Rhonda and Leena had done.

"Leena! You can't barter with the woman. Pay her the $40!" Misha said. "Marilee, can we get going on me, please?"

"I'm not doing anything else until these two pay me," Marilee said.

Misha panicked. Leena took out $35 and handed it to Marilee and walked directly out of the basement salon. "See you later!" she said.

"Misha..." Marilee began.

"I'll take care of it!" Misha said. With that, Rhonda walked out too.

"Take care of mine too, Honey!" Rhonda said to Misha.

"Marilee, OK, I will make it right. Please, just do my hair!"

"OK, first let me get everyone washed and set, it's so much easier to style when I'm not waiting with people at different stages..." and off Marilee bustled with the other four bridesmaids.

When two were under dryers and Marilee was putting rollers in Tamika's hair, Misha and her best woman, Tanya, sat and talked.

"How is this going to work out?" Misha asked, hoping that Marilee wouldn't hear. She was getting pretty mad, but she needed a good style and didn't want to upset Marilee. The last thing she needed was to get tossed out of here with bad hair.

"I think fine. Relax. I'll go hurry things up," Tanya said.

"You sit right back down here! You are only going to make things worse with your big mouth!" Misha told her matron of honor.

"Hmmmph," Tanya said.

Finally, an hour later, it was Misha's turn to get washed and set. It was already 1:30. The wedding was at 5 pm with the limo set to pick them all up at four. There was still so much to do. Misha realized that in all this time she hadn't had anything to eat or drink except for Starbucks the first thing that morning. She was feeling a little nauseated and terribly moody.

"Can we move this thing along?" she asked.

The three girls who'd been dried were lined up for styling, while Misha sat under the dome of the dryer and waited for what seemed like ages. When they were done, the bridesmaids decided to get a bite to eat, and making promises to bring food back, they headed out with their nice up-dos. Each politely paid Marilee before they left. Everyone was a little embarrassed by the way Rhonda and Leena had behaved.

When the three weren't back within the next half hour, Misha was nervous. She prayed as Marilee wound an elaborate up-do involving braids and curls, a French chignon, and a deep, sweeping bang across her forehead. She carefully applied a full air-brush makeup to her fine features and topped off Misha's face with a brownish-rose lipstick.

Finally, she sat the sparkling tiara on the bride's head and spun her around to face the mirror.

"Ta da!" Marilee said.

Misha raised her head slowly and took in her hairstyle and makeup. She burst into tears.

"It's all wrong!" she cried.

Her matron of honor's hair was last, and even with a crying bride, Marilee had to keep moving or no one would be getting to any wedding today. She tossed Misha a box of tissues.

"Tanya, have a seat," she said.

Beginning to comb out the curlers, she said,

"OK Misha, this is what we talked about. What's wrong?"

"It doesn't look right!"

"We looked at pictures – this is what you showed me."

"I hate it! I don't want to look like this in my pictures! I don't want to walk down the aisle like this!" Misha said.

Tanya, staying out of it, wondered aloud, "Where's everybody? Weren't they bringing back food?"

Misha looked at her with eyes on fire.

"Is that all you can think about?"

"Your hair is fine. It is just like the picture you wanted. Now stop being a baby and let this girl do my hair. Text those women and find them. Get them 'unlost' or whatever." Tanya said.

By 3 pm, Tanya was finished, and the three women who'd gone for lunch were finally back, laughing over their adventure. Misha had been calmed by their gasps of pleasure when they saw her hair.

"You look amazing!"

"Oh, my God, let's get you dressed and married off!!"

Misha smiled shyly and apologized for her tantrum earlier.

"I think I have a little low blood sugar from not eating. And wedding jitters," she said.

She thanked Marilee and paid her with a generous tip. She went out to the car with the three bridesmaids while Tanya lagged behind.

"Thanks for texting them with a heads up, Tanya. I think you saved the day!" Marilee said.

"Yeah, it'll be fine unless those women tell Misha that I warned them to be nice!" Tanya said. And she hurried out to help her friend get to a late, but beautiful, wedding.

I know that two of my stories involve girls getting ready, but so many stories revolve around the subject that I really couldn't resist. In this case, budget, timing, and ironing things out in advance with vendors and the attendants would have gone a long way to smoothing the wedding day's all-important preparation.

CHAPTER 49
JUDY'S WEDDING BLUES

I shot Judy's wedding and got to know her pretty well during our meetings prior to the wedding day. She had a few slip-ups, but she was easy-going, and she could have done with a little more due diligence.

Like many little girls, Judy had been planning her dream wedding for what seemed like forever. Now she was twenty-six and right in the middle of real-life wedding planning.

Judy was a laid back computer geek. She did everything online from ordering her flowers to sending out Invites. Judy did most of the work herself, with little help from her fiancé Paul. The only thing they decided on together was the location for their destination wedding. They chose a tropical location because they had met and fallen in love on a beach in the Florida Keys.

Judy found a quaint little Bed and Breakfast by the ocean off the coast of Mexico. She did all of her research on the internet and felt like it was exactly what she was looking for. The pictures on the website displayed a beautiful cottage complete with a garden in the back, where Judy decided she would have the wedding ceremony.

About six months prior to the wedding, Judy made her first and only phone call to the Bed and Breakfast. She asked all the questions she felt she needed to, and was thrilled when they told her that she could pay once she arrived. So, Judy had all the confidence in the world that her honeymoon plans were in place. As far as she was concerned, she was ready to get married!

Two weeks before the wedding, Judy received the dress that she had ordered online. It came in a huge package with beautiful silver wrapping. In her eagerness to get to the package, she turned her ankle on the stairs leading down to the entry where the box had been left. At first, the ankle did not hurt, so she hopped around, getting the box in the house, finding scissors, getting half-undressed in order to try the dress on.

Grabbing the scissors, she started to cut through the box, bending close to examine the dress. Immediately she realized something was wrong. She pulled all the tissue paper out of the way and took a good look at the dress. To Judy's dismay, it did not look anything like the pictures she had pored over. This dress was cream-colored and had some beading on the front, while her dream dress was simple, classic, and quite plain, un-beaded white chiffon. And now, to make matters worse, there was a huge rip in the side bodice where she had used the scissors to cut the box.

Panicking, Judy didn't even consider that perhaps she'd just gotten the wrong dress and it could be easily exchanged. With time running out, Judy was preoccupied with the thought that she would never be able to find a replacement. She would have to settle for this style and color and just get the dress mended. She grabbed the dress and ran to the local tailor to have it stitched up. He told her it would take a few days to be repaired, and she could have the dress fitted once it was done.

That evening, Judy noticed that her ankle was getting bigger. It had become very painful, but Judy felt a good night's sleep was all she needed. By the next morning, her ankle was so swollen; she couldn't even walk on it. So much for the errands she had to run. Paul was busy at work, and Judy was not on speaking terms with her maid of honor at the moment. With no one to ask for help, Judy had no choice but to put off the last-minute errands until the following week – the week of the wedding.

Two days before she and Paul were to leave for Mexico, her ankle was better, and she was able to run the errands she had put off. After picking up some last-minute items for the trip, Judy picked up her wedding dress from the tailor. Once she got it hemmed, she decided to try it on one final time. To her astonishment, the dress did not fit! Judy was distraught. Her only option was to run to the local department store and purchase a new dress – which was not in the budget.

Finding a dress somewhat closer to what she first had in mind, Judy settled for "off the rack" and returned home to pack. Two days later, she and Paul were on the plane.

They landed in Mexico and hopped into a taxi headed toward the Bed and Breakfast. Paul was concerned that Judy had not spoken to the owners in six months, but Judy assured him that everything was fine. She was proved wrong when the taxi arrived at the address; the Bed and Breakfast had closed down. Everything seemed fine on the website last week when she checked. It was a complete shock to Judy.

Paul was furious and let her know how irresponsible she was not to have kept in contact with the B and B owner. Now their entire family was flying down to stay at a place that did not exist. Fishing around for other options, the cab driver told them about a place further down the road. It was a small hotel that had an outdoor restaurant on the beach. Desperate, they rushed over to see if they could work something out.

Fortunately, Judy and Paul were able to book a few hours in the restaurant for the reception, and they were free to use the beach for their ceremony. The only problem was that it was going to cost them way more than they had anticipated. So once again, Judy went over her budget. They scrambled to call family members to let them know about the change of plans.

When the wedding day dawned, chilly and rainy, Judy couldn't do anything but resign herself to an indoor ceremony in a second-rate restaurant.

Judy and Paul had their wedding, but the stress took its toll on Judy, and she didn't enjoy it the way she had wanted. Of course, she should have been keeping regular contact with the Bed and Breakfast. Trusting the internet exclusively was not a smart idea for Judy when it came to the venue or the wedding gown. And, she should have tried on the dress sooner.

Judy's falling out with her maid of honor meant she had no one to help her with her last-minute errands, though she could have asked more of her fiancé. Judy wasn't cutting corners financially or trying to short-cut diligent planning. She simply trusted the internet for the sort of details that should be followed up in person or over the phone – with plenty of room, time, and backup plans to prepare for contingencies that might arise on the way to the "perfect" wedding.

CHAPTER 50
WEDDING NUT

This is a sensitive topic, shared by a friend and probably experienced by more people than we will ever know!

Some brides and grooms put pressure on themselves to look, feel, and perform perfectly on the wedding night. It is a recipe for disaster. Expectations, the long, stressful day, the combination of too little sleep and too much alcohol all conspire to turn romantic fantasies into disappointing failures. You are not alone on your wedding night; all that happens at the end of the day is sleep!

LaMarie was twenty-one and sheltered. She grew up in a conservative, religious household and was very inexperienced with boyfriends.

She met Carlo at a San Gennaro Festival as she waited in line for the Ferris wheel with her friends. Carlo was captivated by the three adorable young women before him, and he invited all three to join him for ice cream after their ride.

He smiled at their childlike innocence and youthful beauty, but his eyes kept returning to LaMarie, the prettiest one of them all. He asked if she had a boyfriend.

"I have boy friends," she said, "but, no, I don't date anyone."

"Maybe I could come by sometime and take you to a movie?" Carlo asked.

"You'd have to ask my father," she said.

Ah, so that's how it is, he thought. Very old-fashioned. He liked it. It was refreshing. More experienced women were fun and exciting, but he liked this new experience, someone without a long past to wade through.

During the year of their courtship, they became close, enjoying many dates, even trips together. Of course, they were intimate with one another but never consummated their relationship.

When Carlo proposed to LaMarie at Christmas of the following year, she excitedly agreed. Of course, Carlo had already asked for LaMarie's hand from her parents at a dinner one night a few weeks before. LaMarie had been helping prepare dinner in the kitchen. Carlo caught her parents alone and swore them to secrecy once they had agreed to the match.

LaMarie would be going straight from her father's strict, religious home to the arms of her husband, a man a bit older than she, and much more worldly than she was. LaMarie had been taught that chastity was a virtue and that a girl must wait until her wedding night to sleep with her groom. Carlo was patient, and he agreed to wait for his bride, though his resolve was often tested during their long courtship. He was determined to love this woman, and so learned her moods, likes and dislikes. He noticed that she had moody times during the month when she didn't want him to touch her – "Don't hang all over me!" She would say angrily. The next day, she would cry and ask him whether or not he loved her.

LaMarie had a difficult time during her monthly periods, but she was modest and found it hard to tell Carlo. She realized he knew what was going on. He came to know that she would get quite sick during that week, with cramping and nausea and extreme tiredness. She didn't like to be stroked or even have her hand held during that time – and she was more irritable than she normally permitted herself to be.

Cheerfulness had been considered a virtue in her home while growing up, so she tried to always put on a good front. When she was sick and moody, however, she withdrew, occasionally snapped at Carlo and would go into feelings of rejection and low-esteem when she would convince herself that Carlo didn't find her beautiful or desirable.

LaMarie had never been on birth control, she had never really had to pay much attention to when her cycle would start. More savvy brides take extra pills to keep their periods at bay so they won't have to worry about it on their wedding nights and for their honeymoons. Others count carefully to schedule the nuptials for "safe times." LaMarie didn't take any of these things into consideration.

As her wedding day approached and all the finalizing of plans had to be taken care of, LaMarie was impatient and nervous. She snapped at Carlo when he drove too slowly and when he forgot what errand was the next on the list. He didn't mind. He was so looking forward to their wedding night – to getting past the wedding event itself. He wanted to be with her – in every way. He wanted to show her his love and attraction so that she would never doubt it again. It didn't cross his mind that LaMarie was getting her period.

The morning of the wedding dawned, overcast and humid. LaMarie woke up achy and weepy. She felt the deep pangs in her abdomen and realized what it meant. She felt groggy and nauseated and couldn't eat anything for breakfast except some weak tea. Her bridesmaids began arriving one by one, and she was listless and didn't want them to fuss over her – not to touch her hair or do her makeup. After several Advil, some coffee, and a hot shower, the bride finally got dressed and conjured up some excitement to get her through the wedding and to her reception.

She told Carlo she wasn't hungry, she lied and said her feet hurt from her high heels. She made all sorts of excuses to be able to sit quietly and talk with her mother or sisters during the wedding reception. Carlo started to understand what was going on. Inside, his frustration grew. Would there be no wedding night? Another week to wait? He had waited for so long – wasn't there something she could have done? At least told him?

LaMarie worried all day about how she would tell Carlo about her period. She feared his reaction because she hated to disappoint him. She wondered if he would make advances and not listen to her reasons why she had to say "no." She'd pushed his hands away so many times, what if he thought she was just playing coy? What an awkward thing to talk to a man about, she thought, then realizing this was her husband, the man who would see her pregnant and in labor, God willing – she resigned herself to telling him the truth.

In their hotel room after everyone had finally gone home to their own beds, Carlo took LaMarie in his arms. She had been terribly nervous and even on the verge of tears.

"Carlo, I am so sorry…" she said.

"Shhh, Darling, it's all right," He said.

A wave of panic passed over her face. "What do you mean?" she asked, as if her secret was already revealed and she wasn't ready for it to be.

"I understand if we have to wait tonight. I am very disappointed, yes. But, I love you so, and I know we have a lifetime together."

"I'm so sorry, Carlo!" she said.

"Silly, there is nothing you could have done. We had a beautiful day, didn't we? Do you feel well? Want some tea? Come; let's look at the cards and texts on our phones."

So they snuggled together on the wedding bed and sipped tea and champagne alternately, bonding instead of brooding, accepting one another, for better and for worse.

Take the pressure off the wedding night, and everyone will be happier. Be sure that it isn't a sign of things to come – not a harbinger of bad luck if all you do is fall into bed exhausted, and go to sleep.

CONCLUSION

Will _Wedding Whoops_ reduce the number of mishaps or "mistakes" that happen on your wedding day? It all depends on whether you are one of those rare people who can learn from someone else's mistakes or if you are like most of us who prefer to make our own, (then look back and wish we'd taken the advice that was handed to us!).

If you can't picture yourself in any of these fifty scenarios, congratulations! You are either perfect or lucky! When it comes to weddings, most of us are stressed and emotional, sensitive to what others will think and nervous as heck.

If you can stop worrying about your own nerves, try to focus on your partner, your friends, loved ones, and even the people you hire for the big day. Treat everyone with care and dignity. Be honest, pay up, give credit where it is due, and be grateful. Apologize, even if you aren't sure if you need to. If you wonder whether an apology is due, it is. If you're in doubt, remember, it's never too soon to say you're sorry but it sure can be too late.

There will be things that don't go according to plan at your wedding. Even brides or grooms who say everything was perfect have probably decided -- either consciously or unconsciously -- to forget about the negatives and focus on the good. In doing this, those wise men and women are laying the groundwork for their married life.

They aren't the exception – they had things go wrong on the big day. But, they are remarkable because instead of holding on to the hurt or anger or regret, they focus on their beloved, the gathering of their friends and family and all the things that went right. They are the flexible and forgiving partners who will make room for mistakes in their relationship and move past them with new insights into how to love and let go and *live*.

One piece of advice I'd add is to make sure you and your partner are in harmony on the wedding day. Obviously, that means more than just not have a shouting match in front of the guests. It also doesn't mean be in agreement on everything – though that would be nice! It means, even if you wind up walking down the aisle barefoot, with a stain on the dress and an empty ring box in your suit pocket, you are smiling into your lover's eyes, ready to enjoy the day anyway.

We become what we do day after day. Maybe you've been engaged for five years or lived together already for ten, but tradition says the wedding day is the first day of your married life. So on this "first" day together, start becoming the easiest husband or wife to live with; the most gracious, the most loving. On that day when you cross the threshold to a new life, let the past be the past: forgive any hurt lingering in the back of your mind. Make it a fresh start.

As for the "big show," let the wedding day be *more* than a spectacle, let it be the symbol of who you will be together - how you will live your married lives. Let your wedding day be the first "task accomplished" in your marriage. Begin to make your history – to write your own story - on this day, going forward.

Wedding Tips

Planning a wedding has the potential to be complicated, but it doesn't have to be! You may feel overwhelmed with all of the organizing, planning and tasks you have to juggle, but not to worry! This useful guide is handy to keep you on track.

First, it is the bridal shower. You may want to have one with your gal pals and make it as unique as you are. To keep it fun, here are some unique bridal shower games.

10 Bridal Shower Games

- Ring Hunt: Before the shower, hide about a dozen plastic rings around the room. Whoever finds the most rings before the end of the shower wins a prize!
- DIY Bridal Shower Clock: Assign each attendee a specific hour ahead of time (maybe in their invitation) and encourage them to pick a gift in line with the time. For example, you could say, "A cup of coffee at nine sounds fine." Then the bride-to-be reads out the notes in chronological order.
- Date Jar: Set up an empty jar with a sign explaining that each guest should write down their suggestions for the perfect "date night" as a newly married couple. Encourage them to go wild! Then the bride can read them at the end of the party, or save them to share with her beloved.

- Name That Cake Game: For a kitchen-inspired bridal shower, guests are asked to think outside the box to figure out a few cake-related riddles.

- How Old Were They Game: This is a great "going down memory lane" game, where the bride puts up pictures of her and the groom at various ages (from baby to the present) and guests try to guess what age they were in the photo. The one with the most correct guesses wins a prize!

- Newlywed "Tip" Jar: The bride will not only take home great marital tips from her fellow girls, but this can also double as a guest book. Have blank pages laid out for them to fill out with their name and their "tip" to put into the jar.

- Oversized Jenga: A great DIY lawn game. A life-size Jenga will have them enthralled and howling with laughter as the game progresses. Make it bridal-themed!

- Paint-by-Numbers: A different take on the traditional bridal shower game routine. Make the afternoon fun and relaxing by setting out jars of numbered paint, creating a few workstations and just let your guests express their creativity.

- Bridal Shower Fortune Teller: This childhood favorite can be transformed into a fun adult game for a nostalgia-inspired shower. This is the origami-style game where you choose a panel and lift the paper to see your fortune. Add a few questions related to her own childhood to make it special.

- Emoji Pictionary: Anyone with a smartphone will get a kick out of this game, where the work's already done for you! Simply download and print!

5 Ways to Select your Wedding Vendors

It's important to select the best vendors to breathe life into your wedding day vision! You have many options and it can be overwhelming. But if you take it step by step, you will own the process and be on top of it. First, schedule appointments with the vendors you are interested in. These include:

- A Videographer/photographer
- Church ceremony venue/wedding reception venue
- Catering/bar vendor
- Florist
- DJ/Musical band service
- Bridal gown/tux

Start with an initial phone call to get the basics out of the way, well in advance. This alone will help you weed out vendors who do not fit your budget or may be unavailable on your wedding day. Then, when you meet face to face, dress as you would for a meeting at work (i.e. no sweats or jeans.) Respect the vendor's time and hear them out, even if you know within five minutes that they are not "the one."

1. Get with your fiancé and set a budget, then do your homework beforehand (see wedding budget above.) How big do you want your wedding to be? You

don't want to fall in love with a venue if it is too large or small to accommodate your guests. As you start to comparison shop, you will soon get a clearer picture of all associated costs. Come prepared with questions and don't get carried away as you get "wooed" by all of their great services!

2. Determine during the face-to-face if your personalities mesh well with the vendor. Did you establish a quick rapport with them? Do they make you feel comfortable? Remember, you will be entrusting them with the service they provide during a very emotional day for you. If anything about them feels "off", trust your gut, they may not be the best choice.

3. Client referrals. Don't be shy about asking for them. Check out other brides' testimonials, and directly ask the vendor to provide contact info of recent clients who can vouch for their service. Just don't forget to pay it forward by writing great reviews and/or providing info for future brides!

4. Get everything in writing down to the last detail. Vendors should itemize everything that is included in the price. If they don't, ask for it! Take the florist, for example. If you know exactly what kind of flower(s) you want, make sure that is clearly stated in their itemized contract. This information will protect you in the event of a dispute or in the event

the items are not available during that time. Look for any hidden costs and ask for clarification on anything that doesn't make sense to you.

5. Don't hesitate to negotiate! If their services come in a bundle and you don't think you'll need all of them, ask if they can offer a discount for those services you don't want or need. Or negotiate to take advantage of them at a later date. Also, vendors that offer more than one service (e.g. photographer and music) may be able to cut you a deal if you use them for both. Just remember, kindness goes a LONG way!

The purpose of this book is to equip the millennial couples the fundamentals of wedding day, also to be a learning examples from these 50 couples from all over the world.
As a wedding videographer, I have seen before, during and after every wedding day I have shot, couple with the research i made from other wedding day trauma.

I believe this book will help you to finally focus your energy on your mate for this marital journey.
Let your wedding story count.

Congratulation!!!
Thank you.

Made in the USA
Middletown, DE
15 April 2023

28840719R00146